A Practical Guide for Managing
Adolescent Addiction
to Digital Devices

by Harris Kern and Ina D'Aleo

© Copyright 2016 Harris Kern and Ina D'Aleo

ISBN 978-1-63393-330-9

Published by

◄ köehlerbooks™

210 60th Street
Virginia Beach, VA 23451
800-435-4811
www.koehlerbooks.com

A Practical Guide For Managing

ADOLESCENT ADDICTION

To Digital Devices

Harris Kern & Ina D'Aleo

author of over 40 books

with a foreword written by Dr. Joseph Avant, Ph.D.

VIRGINIA BEACH

CAPE CHARLES

Table of Contents

Dedicated to
My 18-Year-Old Daughter Alexandria (Alex)

"My last major goal was to see you happy and successful before I left this planet. You were ADDICTED to your cellular, even falling asleep with it in your hand every night. You lived in a virtual world engulfed in social media and other apps accessed by your smartphone, and coupled with your horrific misuse of time, highly emotional state, poor self-discipline, lack of key life skills and no urgency to excel as an adult, contributed heavily to your naiveté and immaturity. However, I never blamed you. My negligence to mentor you in key life skills was my fault. Although it was quite a taxing ordeal to cope with your issues and arm you with the proper skills for adulthood. . . we did it.

Thank you for fulfilling my last goal, Alex.

I love you.

Daddy

(Harris Kern)

Foreword

The Experience of Technology

Written by Dr. Joseph Avant, Ph.D

Harris Kern has spent his life devoted to helping others help themselves through prudent self-discipline. This book, more so than any of his others, continues that lifelong commitment. In fact, this book represents a kind of culmination of it. Allow me the following few pages to explain what I mean by this in distinguishing the underlying and fundamental difference Harris articulates in this book between mere moralizing and the much more serious activity of rigorously engaging in leadership through self-discipline.

All adult professionals know too well the consequences of performing poorly in their careers, maintaining a good health regimen, and their most personal relationships. The manifest awareness of these consequences comes from the everyday life experiences of simply being an adult. For example, in the same way we have all had to learn that we are best served in our financial decisions by becoming informed consumers, we have also had to learn that we are similarly best served in our dealings with others by becoming better informed about our own opinions and, consequently, the need to reflect upon them in order to sufficiently justify them. The principal reason for this is simply that we have had to learn from our own experiences that it is from our opinions that we guide our most important actions in life. Indeed, the difference between mere opinions and educated opinions is nowhere more consequential than in one's everyday practical decisions. Such knowledge gleaned from our experiences comes only through time. Unfortunately, this is precisely the reason why those who need it most are lacking in it. That is, sufficient awareness to the full extent of the consequences attendant upon poor performance is anything but manifest to young persons today except, perhaps, through their involvement in sports. This book attempts to correct this all too prevalent deficiency in the skill set of young persons today. In a word, Harris' lifelong journey of helping others to help themselves through prudent self-discipline has led him into the trenches of what will become the legacy of us all, namely our future generations from the adolescents and young adults of today.

Having said that, it might all sound rather clichéd or obvious, but it must never be forgotten that experience teaches all of us that common sense isn't so common after all. That is, while we almost always know what needs to be done in any given situation, it is also true that we almost always fail to act on that knowledge by diligently implementing it in the given situation. The result is that while nothing is given more freely than our own advice, we nonetheless remain poor students of it in our own lives. Enter Harris. Through his various books and life-mentoring engagements Harris provides step-by-step approaches and examples of imminently practical daily guidelines for cultivating productive self-discipline such that it becomes habitual. That is, Harris is a guide for those seeking to break free from the cycle of knowing what to do, but failing to do it. Such an audience is truly, albeit in various degrees, all of us. Yet the significance of Harris' endeavor to further accomplish that task in this book simply cannot be overstated for the following reasons. On its most practical level, the significance of instituting self-discipline in young people is that employers look for three primary characteristics from prospective employees. Employers want to know that their employees can think well, communicate well, and read well.

Attaining the unity of these three characteristics to perform at the highest level is simply impossible without rigorous self-discipline. Moreover, on a deeper and much more important level, the significance of instituting self-discipline in young people is that its implementation is seen the whole world over as that which is most characteristic of leadership—the virtue which is everywhere and always in high demand. In other words, at its highest level Harris' continuous efforts to provide thoughtful persons with counsel and guidance in self-discipline are the characteristics upon which all other virtues depend. Indeed, it is no overstatement to say that what Harris provides is precisely that which we search for and praise most in everything from successful businessmen, locally elected officials, and especially the statesmen we elect to safeguard and manage our country. Accordingly, if virtue is to be imitated from the top down then, as Harris recognizes and demonstrates in these pages, it must be taught from the bottom up.

The issue Harris sets on the table for discussion here is the way in which our youth today is being affected by technology. Now, it is certainly true that educators are rapidly implementing technology in their classrooms to facilitate the education of young people today. However, it is simply undeniable that technology in the form of "social media" is working against our educators despite their best efforts. For example, "texting" has resulted in the birth of a new language rife with acronyms. Compounding this is the way in which word limitations placed upon "tweets" have made eloquence in the articulation of one's thoughts all but impossible. Thus, while our educators are attempting to teach young people how to better communicate their thoughts, the technology our youth is awash in outside of their classrooms is teaching them how to miscommunicate their thoughts in that newfound and uncharted land of "social media." In short, the formal education of young people today is being eroded in a wholesale manner by technology outside of the classroom in the school of life.

The veritable rapidity with which all forms of social media are being created and improved upon is astonishingly greater than that which reaches them in the classrooms of their schools and universities. Indeed, the entire phenomenon of social media represents the culmination of living wholly in the moment through self-publishing even the most trivial minutes of one's daily activities through venues like Face book, Instagram, and Snapchat for the approval of others. Now, the immediate question here is why such self-publication is so powerful and, in fact, addictive. To put it bluntly and rather simply, it's just pleasant to know that others find our lives interesting. The problem, however, is that the more and more one gets caught up and wholly entangled in living in the immediate moment— the proverbial "here and now—the more and more one radically severs oneself from focused attentiveness and deliberation upon the very few but extremely more important activities of daily life which contribute most significantly to a successful and happy future. What Harris provides for educators and parents of young persons in this book is twofold: (1) a means of recognizing such addictions *as* addictions, and (2) practical methods for approaching the tasks of everyday life oriented by the knowledge that one must endure self-discipline today in order that one not suffer regrets tomorrow. In short, precisely because all things excellent are as difficult as they are rare, it is to our great benefit that Harris has provided this book as a guide for us who, destined to being thoughtful persons, might otherwise not know where to turn for guidance in learning how to lead young persons away from the fleeting pleasures of the moment toward habituating them in the otherwise unpleasant, but crucially important endurance of self-discipline for much greater and more enduring pleasures of the future. The journey of a thousand miles begins with a single footstep and continues by simply placing one foot in front of the other. Harris here provides us with the content needed to orient and inform those steps from beginning to end.

With that in mind, let us now speak a bit more precisely about the matter at hand in order to better clarify it and distinguish it from our preconceived understandings of it. In order to do this, we must first come to an agreement regarding terminology. Generally speaking, science is knowledge gained from the study of nature, whereas technology is the application of that knowledge for the benefit of human life. As Americans we are a practical lot, and indeed, the first American contribution to

Western philosophy was aptly named "pragmatism." So to say that technology is not, as it were, all sunshine and rainbows may initially strike us as rather paradoxical. This initial perplexity is in no small measure due to the way in which technology is literally sold to us through technology itself. For example, in everything from television commercials marketing prescription drugs directly and indiscriminately to the public effectively doing away with a physician's counsel to television shows and movies presenting us with wondrous technological conveniences which give reasons for why our lives are better than those of our parents, our own youth, and extending right up to last year, last month, and perhaps even last night. And so is it any wonder why we simply take it for granted that "new and improved" is always better than "old and obsolescent?" Yet it must never be forgotten that when everything is presented as advancing through improvements toward ever-greater things only dreamed of in the past, even and especially things undreamed of in the past, then the awareness of things which endure amid the flux of time can easily become forgotten and perhaps altogether lost. The significance of this for what Harris provides in this book is that when the emphatic goal of technology is to make every aspect of our lives easier, it transpires that the skill of habituating oneself in rigorous self-discipline is occluded in such a way that even when it is recognized as valuable, its value is understood in a diluted way at best and unnecessary at worst. The corrective teaching to this state of affairs that Harris provides here is that technology does not exist for its own sake but for ours, and precisely because of the blurring of this distinction with the advent of social media, there is a very serious question about the value of possessing that which provides us with the best things in life when in doing so, it brings out the worst things in ourselves.

In order to drive this last point home, consider the following. We all know the story of Frankenstein. Yet what very few know is that the author—Mary Shelley—was a brilliant student of Greek tragedy. In fact, her subtitle for the book is "Prometheus Unbound." The reference is to the Greek myth of the god Prometheus giving the knowledge of how to make fire to mankind and with which the whole of technology was born. In other words, Shelley's story is a very thinly veiled critique of and warning against the power of modern science and technology. In a word, even the wisest among us can become monsters when not sufficiently recognizing the way in which our creations can become monstrous despite our best intentions. Let us take two examples. Consider the prospect of being part of the largest, fastest growing, and hands down most profitable technological industry on the planet. Who wouldn't want to be a part of that! Now consider that the industry is Internet pornography. The greatest financially successful industry in the history of human existence produced by the application of knowledge for the benefit of human life is none other than that which is most associated with shame the world over. Isn't that strange? Similarly, and much more immediately devastating, is that not only has technology provided us with the means of corrupting ourselves morally, it has also provided us with the very easy capacity to destroy the entirety of human existence in a grand wholesale manner with nuclear weaponry. The application of knowledge for the benefit of human life has, irony of ironies, provided us with the means of ending the entirety of human existence by merely pressing a single button.

The underlying problem is that the power of science is akin to a blind giant. It can achieve the tasks it sets itself to with profoundly successful efficiency. Yet, it can say nothing to whether or not the tasks are moral, advantageous, or simply evil. That is, even and perhaps especially despite the logo for the software giant Apple, science has not tasted of the forbidden fruit to know the difference between right and wrong. That distinction is wholly left to us and especially the youth to whom we will bequeath our questionable successes. Moreover, as the examples just mentioned make perfectly clear, distinctions of right and wrong can become horribly obscured when monetary or political interests become contributing factors in our deliberation. Granting that these two examples represent extreme cases of the influence of technology in our lives and, as such, do not occupy a significant portion of our thoughts on any given day, they are nonetheless important insofar as they present us with the extremes from which we can begin to better gauge the adverse ways in which technology influences our much more immediate and everyday lives—the "little things," as it were, which constitute our work days and reside far below the horizon of pornographic addiction and nuclear holocaust, but whose culminating effects can be just as devastating, if not worse.

Worse? Well, based strictly, albeit simply, on the numbers alone, one must reconcile the marketing claims made by the technology industry with the fact that since 1988 the rate of antidepressant use in the United States has increased almost 400%. And so if it truly is the case that the quality of our lives increases according to the amount of technology we inject into them, then, to say the least, it isn't reflected by the diagnoses we are receiving from our doctors. That being said, and since the hallmark of our culture is increasingly reflected by our insatiable consumption of technology, then perhaps our culture has much more to tell us about ourselves and our relation to technology than we are sufficiently aware. Such is the stuff, I suggest, from which our deepest longings are both reflected from and informed by. I am speaking of our music and the way in which it reaches into us and helps us articulate the whole host of passions we feel most poignantly.

On March 27, 2000 the Nation Public Radio did a special on the song "Once in a Lifetime" by the popular '80s alternative rock group The Talking Heads as part of its 100 most important American musical works of the 20th century. As indicated by the repetitive use of "and," the song begins in exactly the same way we find ourselves at any given moment, which is to say always already in the middle of things with presuppositions which have unwittingly or insufficiently escaped our attention:

> *And you may find yourself living in a shotgun shack*
> *And you may find yourself in another part of the world*
> *And you may find yourself behind the wheel*
> *of a large automobile*
> *And you may find yourself in a beautiful house,*
> *with a beautiful wife*
> *And you may ask yourself. . . Well. . .*
> *How did I get here?*

At issue is the way in which anyone in any walk of life can very easily go about his or her daily life in activities and the pursuit of things not fully thought through or merely "half-heartedly."

The danger in this is when we do so without even being aware that we haven't thought our purposes through or that we are in fact only acting half-heartedly in pursuit of them. As a result, many people are living lives in which they are simply settling for things which are in fact unsatisfying substitutes for that which they truly long for. In other words, the danger is that one may have become lost in life without ever having recognized that one had gone astray. In unwittingly having become comfortable living a half-hearted life, many have simply been:

Letting the days go by
Let the water hold me down
Letting the days go by
Water flowing underground
Into the blue again
After the money's gone
Once in a lifetime
Water flowing underground

These verses encapsulate an anecdote that is worth remembering: The fish are the last to learn that they live in the sea. In such instances the shock of "find[ing] yourself" can be terrifying:

And you may ask yourself
How do I work this?
And you may ask yourself
Where is that large automobile?
And you may tell yourself
This is not my beautiful house!
And you may tell yourself
This is not my beautiful wife!
And you may ask yourself
What is that beautiful house?
And you may ask yourself
Where does that highway go to?
And you may ask yourself
Am I right? Am I wrong?
And you may say to yourself
My God! What have I done?

In asking "What have I done?" the song has returned to the question asked at the end of the first stanza, "Well. . . How did I get here?" The two questions taken together summarize quite well why it is important to reflect upon technology. The hallmark of technology in our everyday life is witnessed in everything from cell phones, TV applications that can provide access to every television show ever made, and most especially the entire world in which one can spend an entire lifetime known as "social media." Specifically, it provides entertainment in the form of distracting oneself from the things of one's own life that one would simply rather avoid for the time being. This kind of "escapism" is completely understandable because life truly is quite often "a bitch," and technology allows us temporary escapes from it in which we can imagine our life as something other than it is in spectacular fashion. Yet as indicated, this becomes profoundly problematic when the lulling effect of doing so causes one to lose sight of the need to live in accord with one's deepest longing rather than half-heartedly acting one's way through a life in which one would simply rather be distracted by imagined fantasies or merely the lives of others.

I suggest that the most eloquent statement of the understanding of life which can safeguard one from the darker side of technology was penned over 400 years ago. In the penultimate paragraph of the final essay of the collection of essays written to explain himself to the world in order that others might profit from what he had learned, Montaigne wrote the following:

> *"It is an absolute perfection and virtually divine to know how to enjoy our existence rightfully. We seek other conditions in life because we do not understand the use of our own, and we go outside of ourselves because we do not know the treasures to be found inside of ourselves. Yet there is no use of our mounting on stilts, for on stilts we must still walk with our own legs. And on the loftiest throne in the world we are still sitting on our own ass."*

It is worth noting that he titled the essay "Of Experience." And so while there is simply no denying that technology provides us with a quality of life unknown to all civilizations in the history of humanity, it also provides us with a striking opportunity of assessing what is best in us precisely because it does not admit of innovation and, hence, most worthy of our vigilant awareness at a time when claims of progress and innovation in everything go unchallenged. In sum and in short, we are at a sufficiently revealing point in our experience with technology from which we can understand and truly appreciate the wisdom of that which Montaigne sought to teach us from his own experience of a world wholly lacking our technology.

Introduction

ALL CIRCUITS ARE BUSY

** News Flash to Parents**

Your teens aren't prepared for adulthood when they celebrate their eighteenth birthday.

Being an overachiever, accomplishing a great deal and leaving behind a legacy earned me the prestigious successful label from my family, clients, friends, and colleagues. I was extremely disciplined and always strategizing to improve in every facet of my life. I never thought about today (tactically); my obligations on any given day were already written down on my to-do list. I constantly strategized on how to complete my major goals faster by being more efficient and accomplishing more each day in my professional world, health regimen, and relationships with God and my family. The only way to advance one's standing in order to achieve that successful label was to consistently strategize and execute with urgency.

Being distracted by technology 24 hours a day and still operating in slow motion as if time were infinite like many teens do is a recipe for failure as they cross the threshold to adulthood. They're preoccupied on their devices and the virtual world they access. It irked me to watch our youth waste so many hours. I felt that this new age of addictive behavior was handcuffing our youth to their technology and wasting their livelihood in the now, as opposed to thinking strategically for personal and professional improvement.

Unfortunately I was consumed with accomplishing my goals and leaving behind a legacy. I kept ignoring this colossal problem until it hit home—my daughter Alex's 18th birthday was my call to action. I was also caught up in my *Daddy's little girl* representation for years, and suddenly *the day of reckoning* arrived. Alex was now officially an adult. The *day* I was subconsciously avoiding for years arrived.

Alex is a beautiful, loving, and caring individual with an awesome personality and a heart of gold, but she hasn't matured at the same rate as her body. Her mental development lagged behind her physical attributes, which is common among teenage girls. She's lived a sheltered life: hidden from much negativity and raised in an affluent neighborhood. However, she was extremely naive, with low self-esteem, no self-discipline, and was hooked on her cellular like alcoholics are addicted to their bottle. She was addicted to her digital world, based on the definition of addiction: *the fact or condition of being addicted to a particular substance, thing, or activity.*

She wasted an enormous amount of time babbling with friends, futzing with social media, and if she had an unlimited data plan on her cellular, she would be distracted further by downloading apps and playing games galore. Due to her upbringing, she was prepped and protected from the typical front-page types of issues like drugs, STDs, sexuality, bullying, self-identity crisis, independence, and peer pressure, but not so much on the harsh realities, responsibilities, and skills required for thriving as an adult. She had a woman's body and was gifted with a pretty face, but unfortunately her maturity level equaled that of a 15-year-old. She wasn't ready although society said she was, and her friends hyped their new title frequently, notwithstanding she wasn't ready.

The family celebration ended with an enjoyable dinner at a Chinese restaurant. However, as I looked over at my little girl who was fixated on her Smartphone and texting uncontrollably, which in the past I shrugged off as childish nonsense, has now been elevated to a major problem and a deterrent to success. She was addicted to her cellular in a bad way. Whether it was drugs, alcohol or Smartphone usage, all of these bad habits are difficult to break, and all three could kill. Now that may seem a bit far-fetched to some, but most of you reading this book know how challenging life can be, and raising teens without interjecting reality back into their virtual world could cause them to fall hard, and some may never get back up again.

I blame myself and assume full responsibility for my negligence. I didn't prepare her for adulthood, but I wasn't alone; most parents are in the same situation. I had to get involved quickly, but it wasn't going to be easy. The traditional way of parent/child one-direction "do-this" discussion wasn't going to cut it.

Due to the evolution of technology (post-Internet), smartphones and social media have changed the playing field drastically. I'm not suggesting you avoid technology, and I'm not saying it's bad; on the contrary, it's awesome. I use my smartphone profusely for business, banking, and entertainment (managing my stereo system throughout the house). Technology used in moderation, just like everything else, is good. I was desperate because I've seen too many people fail, and I know how difficult it is to achieve success. I felt like the odds of Alex failing the course of Adulthood 101 was extremely high unless I intervened and quickly. I designed a strategy for her, but also to use on other teens I was mentoring in my life coaching profession to wean them off of their addictions to live a more balanced lifestyle and use technology as a catalyst for success.

Can teens succeed on their own? Perhaps, but do you want to take that chance with your child? Adulthood is hard enough without these challenges; it takes a plan, structure, continuous effort, and a mentor to provide guidance and hold them accountable. It starts with you. Look in the mirror; have you accomplished your goals, how many hours a day do you waste, do you wake up with a purpose and live life with passion, urgency and follow a healthy routine? I already know that the answer to most of these questions is a resounding *no*. What you've been struggling with most of your life will only get worse for your teen. Help them overcome and succeed by teaching them the skills highlighted in this book. Are you up for the challenge?

How Bad Was My Daughter's Addiction

As a former IT executive and avid smartphone owner, technology advances have been incredible. It has truly made our lives fun and interesting if utilized in a controlled manner.

Unfortunately with most teens it is abused, and they become addicted, like my daughter:

- It caused sleep deprivation. She fell asleep with it in her hand every night. Unfortunately, it was always on. She never turned it off, which meant on many occasions calls and texts occurred in the middle of the night.
- Her memory was horrible because she was constantly being distracted and was more worried about the next text message than her priorities.
- She lived in a virtual world most of the time— fantasyland, which contributed to her naiveté.
- She didn't utilize sufficient resources to strategize about her future.
- She couldn't put her cellular down. Even in our media room, we had a rule during movies, just like in movie theatres—all devices off. I would have to yell at her to turn it off.
- It contributed to her laziness.
- She abused time like there was an infinite amount.
- She lacked proper social abilities. She didn't communicate effectively.

These issues severely impacted Alex's development. I remember on one particular night, two months shy of her 18th birthday, I picked her up from work, and upon our arrival home around 11 p.m., she informed me that she left her cellular at work. I told her we would pick it up in the morning before school. She initiated such a stink because she wanted to go back and pick up her phone. I said no because it was a 15-minute drive, and I was exhausted. I stood my ground, and a big brouhaha ensued. It's like she was having major withdrawals, as if she were a drug addict and couldn't get a fix that she desperately needed—unbelievable.

In *The Washington Post* article *"Teens say they're addicted to technology. Here's how parents can help,"* the author Amy Joyce states that according to a new report of Common Sense Media, *50 percent of teens* actually admitted that they feel addicted. Just imagine what the real number is. Not only do teens feel that they can't put their devices down, but their parents know it (59 percent), and many parents themselves can't put their own devices down (27 percent).

Based on the report, teens feel their parents are addicted as well. For instance, *48 percent of parents* feel they have to answer emails and texts immediately, and *72 percent of teens* say they need to; *69 percent of parents* say they check devices hourly, while *78 percent of teens* do.

The report also found that screens are impacting our health and safety: *56 percent of parents* admit to using devices while driving—with kids in the car – and *51 percent of teens* see their parents checking mobile devices while driving (*The Washington Post*, 2016).

Overview

A Practical Guide For Managing Adolescent Addiction To Digital Devices has been written to arm parents (you) with the formula: strategy, roadmap, and skills required to help teens thrive as adults. My objectives of this book are:

1. Reduce the obsession to smartphones and the virtual playground where most teens habitat and navigate for gaming, texting for hours, and utilizing an excessive amount of time on social media.
2. Develop the skills, structure, and self-discipline to thrive and maintain a balanced lifestyle by focusing on their priorities.
3. Utilize technology as a catalyst to be more productive and efficient.

This book's content is gender neutral and divided into four main sections. The first three sections are dedicated to helping parents teach adolescents (ages 13-18) the most critical adulthood skills they will need to be successful. Section four is written by Ina D'Aleo, a teacher and mother of a thirteen-year-old son residing in New York City. It is specifically written for parents who are trying to raise children (ages 2-12) with structure, self-discipline, and keeping them technologically hungry, but addiction-free.

The frustration of watching teens (including my daughter) glued to their cellular and watching this resource-exhaustive addiction dictate their life was eating me alive. As a self-development expert and someone who walks the talk, I know what the human body and mind are capable of. It was time to share that knowledge with other parents. I also helped as many teens as I could via my life coaching profession. Below is a representation of each section.

I. The Strategy

Section I depicts the big picture—the strategy for transitioning teens to adults. The key components of my methodology are:

- Establishing a partnership built on trust and camaraderie
- Utilizing unique communication practices such as reverse psychology, among others
- Assessing strengths and weaknesses to provide a gap analysis, get buy-in, and set expectations
- Identifying and developing adulthood skills based on the top priorities
- Being a mentor and promoting key principles
- Discussing how to broker a deal to move forward
- Executing with urgency
- Building a foundation by instituting structure and setting goals with milestones

It's definitely an exhaustive and resource-intense effort to execute this strategy, but it does work and the rewards are immeasurable.

II. Develop Vital Adulthood Skills

Section II highlights the skills required for adulthood. Your teen can be a scholastic genius, but without these crucial life skills their odds for success in an adult world are minimal. I focus on the top priorities: finances, career, health, and relationships. Expertise needs to be developed to succeed in these important categories. I provide the minimum, yet sufficient prescriptions for transitioning your teen to adulthood.

III. Your Teen's Life, Inc.

This section describes the life plan (roadmap) I utilized and how you can be a mentor and help transition your teen into a successful adult. The mentoring will be excruciatingly difficult and resource exhaustive. I am not going to sugarcoat the effort. The odds of them learning these skills effectively on their own are slim, and if they mean the world to you as my daughter does to me, then don't just buy them a car and pretend you're a good parent; be a mentor and help them learn these valuable skills.

IV. The Roles of Technology in Education and at Home

Section IV was conceived to help you teach children (ages 2-12) technology's role in education and what are the do's and don'ts of technology to ensure your children's safety while developing their technological skills. It was written by Ina D'Aleo. This section also highlights how the family plays a major role in monitoring Internet usage, so you can prevent addiction to games and social media at an early age. If it's already too late, how do you wean your children off their texting, video games, and social media addiction?

Throughout the book I have implanted numerous case studies from not only my coaching business, but from my personal experiences with my daughter. Below are depictions of two teens I coached professionally.

Real Life Scenario: The Whiz Kid

Zane (fictitious name) was one of those genius whiz kids who loved to tinker with electronics. At the age of sixteen he built a robot that won him first place in an international robotics competition. When he graduated from high school, he was awarded a scholarship to a prestigious school in Massachusetts which specialized in robotics.

Zane knew he was a genius when it came to electronics so he didn't have to try very hard to ace his robotics class; unfortunately he took that same lackadaisical attitude with all of his other classes. He rarely applied himself in other subjects that were required to get his Bachelor's degree. His GPA after his first semester was disastrous; he actually flunked his Physics class. That's when his mom contacted me in a panic.

Unfortunately Zane was addicted to video games and social media. He would stay up most of the night and would even skip out on having lunch at school to get back on Face book and Snapchat to be with his online buddies. He was antisocial: an introvert who couldn't communicate well in front of real people, only with the ones in his virtual world—his comfort zone. He was an addict of the worst kind, being online probably 8-10 hours a day.

Zane was an only child raised by his mom. His dad physically abused him when he was young. His mom finally left his dad, but Zane was already scarred—she was trying her hardest to help him overcome the past and excel in school. She tried everything before contacting me, which included tutors, threatened to take his computer away, took him to psychiatrists, blamed it on ADD, etc. She was desperate, I was her last hope. I said, "This was going to be a huge undertaking because your son has some major problems, including his addiction to video games." The only way I would mentor Zane was if he acknowledges his addiction and works with me to overcome it.

"I understand." She said.

The next day I began working with Zane and started probing immediately. We had our first of many SKYPE sessions. We discussed his goals, strengths, and weaknesses. It was also important to write them down so he could visually see that his weaknesses were triple the size of his strengths. I asked him point blank, without any sugarcoating:

"Do you think you can accomplish one of your major goals, which is becoming a CEO of a robotics company with those weaknesses?"

He quickly said, "No, sir."

I had his full attention. I decided to put it all out on the table and not hold anything back. *"Physically, you look terrible. You have absolutely no muscle tone, and you're scrawny. Do you like the way you look?"*

"No, sir, I don't."

That's what I wanted to hear. *"Are you ready to make sacrifices and change your current mode of operation to accomplish your goals?"*

"Yes, sir, I am."

"This isn't going to be easy; you know that—right?"

"Yes, sir, I know that."

"I also need a copy of your class schedule for the week before we start."

"Okay, I will get that to you later today."

"That nonsense of being up all night playing video games with your virtual buddies needs to stop. Are you okay with that?"

"Yes, sir, I have no choice."

Although he agreed, he had no idea how difficult this endeavor would be, primarily due to the severity of his addiction. Anyone can say they agree, but putting forth the effort to change is a whole different ball game.

"Okay, let's come up with a plan and get your life on track as quickly as possible."

We followed the strategy highlighted in the next section, which included setting realistic goals, with milestones for each goal, and a new morning and evening routine to focus more on his studies, family obligations (helping his mom), and exercise. One of his new health-related goals was to become more muscular. I started the mentoring process and watched over him like a hawk watches over its prey. I would call or text him throughout the day, especially before or after the classes he was previously failing. During our Skype sessions we worked on training his mind by repeating negative phrases to combat his addiction and lack of urgency. The phrases he chose were hardcore, but he had no choice. He had to get tough on himself to make up for lost time in a hurry. His favorite phrase was: "I'm a pathetic loser. Do I want to be this piece of crap for the rest of my life?"

After a several months his confidence level soared as he was acing his exams and feeling great about his weightlifting routine. The larger his muscles grew, the more confidence he gained. He turned his life around. Over the next few years he aced college.

Real Life Scenario: Overcoming Drugs, Privilege, Abuse, and Laziness

David was seventeen years old and starting his senior year of high school. He was another one of those scholastically gifted kids that wasted time like there was an infinite amount. He was hooked on video games, but also smoked marijuana every day—just like his dad who was an attorney, although his father used it for medicinal purposes; I found out later that his dad had a rare disease that was terminal.

David was spoiled; besides being able to get his hands on as much marijuana as he could possibly consume, his parents were well off and they bought him anything he wanted, including a brand new car the instant he received his driver's license. David was also lazy. He didn't want to do anything around the house, which included not cleaning his room, not picking up after himself anywhere in the house, and lounging in bed for hours at a time. He also swore profusely—mostly at his mom. He was a real piece of work.

Scholastically he was sporting a B average without even trying. David's mom (Mary) was desperate, so she contacted me. I told Mary that I would have to meet with David to determine if he really wanted to change. She agreed, and the following day, which was Sunday, I drove to her house. There was no time to waste, but before I officially engaged with David, I wanted him to be comfortable around me. His mom mentioned that he loved playing football with his buddies, so when I arrived at his house, the first thing we did was toss the ball around for about thirty minutes. He had an awesome arm and could heave that football a long way. After playing, we went inside and sat alone on the couch in the living room, and I asked him:

"What do you want to do with your life when you graduate?"

"I'd like to get into sports management."

"Cool, are you going to college?"

"Yup," as he was nodding his head up and down.

Then I got right to the point. *"Why do you think your mom contacted me?"*

"Probably because I'm lazy, take drugs, play video games all day, and treat her like crap."

"Is that it?"

"That pretty much sums it up."

"Do you know much about me?"

"I Googled you, and I saw that you wrote a lot of books."

"Yes, but we can discuss all of that later. You've got a good football arm; do you have other goals you'd like to pursue?"

"Thanks, I'd like to earn the starting quarterback position on my school's football team in my senior year. Tryouts are in a few months and then hopefully get recruited and play in college, too."

"Okay, sounds good, so tell me what are some of your strengths besides having a good football arm?"

"I'm smart; schoolwork comes easy. I also have a bunch of friends, so I guess I get along with people easily."

"Okay, sounds good, now I'll tell you my strengths." I rambled off a few as he looked at me with amazement. *"I'll even tell you my weaknesses,"* which I preceded to tell him. *"Can you tell me any additional weaknesses?"*

"I don't apply myself in school, waste time, and I smoke too much weed."

"Okay, I got the picture; hey, at least your honest. I have one last question for you; do you want to change, David? Before you answer, let me add that changing the current David won't be easy. We basically have to kill the old David, but he won't go away easily."

"I don't have a choice, I don't want to be a failure for the rest of my life."

Then I threw an old copy of Hot Rod Magazine on the couch beside him. It was me on the front cover in the July 1975 issue. Most male teens love muscle cars, and I had the grandest ride of them all. "That was my tricked-out car and speedboat combo, which were painted identical maroon with flames." It was unparalleled for a 21-year-old to accomplish that much at such a young age.

He said, "Wow, sweet."

Then I threw one of my books in the same spot the magazine was in and said, "I've published over 40 books. The choice is yours, David; you can continue to be a loser and squeak through your senior year and amount to nothing or make something out of your life. Either way, I am leaving right now, but feel free to call me if you want to change."

As I stood up, he looked at me and said, "Please help me."

"Are you sure?"

"Yes, I don't want to be a loser."

Over the next week, we established goals: attain straight A's, become the starting quarterback, stop smoking weed, and control his addiction to video games. We also established milestones for each goal along with a new morning and evening routine.

"I will be contacting you daily to make sure you stay on track and stopping by several times a week so we can straighten out your life in a hurry. Oh, and there's one more thing: disrespecting your mother stops today."

"Yes, sir."

Things changed immediately for David. His priorities were his studies first every day, followed by strength training at the gym and tossing that football around, as football tryouts were fast approaching. He also wanted to retake the SAT exam during his senior year because he got a horrible score during his junior year. His new daily routine included SAT studies. He also stopped badmouthing his mother, cleaned up after himself around the house, and got a part-time job to start earning his own way in life.

Over the course of his senior year, he was sporting a 4.45 GPA, and his new SAT score was 1920. What a transformation . . . He also became the starting quarterback in his senior year of high school. He was recruited by the UCLA football program in Los Angeles.

I was very proud of David, and so was his mom, to say the least. Were there bumps along the way? Sure, he was a teenager, and when he messed up, I let him know. I held him accountable daily to his obligations and goals.

The Issues Summarized

Technology has been challenging, exciting, and rewarding for over four decades. I was practically raised in Information Technology, hired by a large company in Silicon Valley, California. My official job title was Burstor/Decollator. It was an entry-level position in their Data Processing Department. I was eighteen years old back in 1972, when I was taking carbon out of the reams of paper that were being printed daily. After a few months I was promoted into that coveted computer room, operating that giant IBM mainframe. When powered on, it looked like a giant square Christmas tree with red, green, and white lights on the front panel. I'll never forget the day IBM rolled in their latest and greatest mainframe onto our newly built computer room with a raised floor and glass walls, officially labeled a Data Center.

Hardware and software advances have been unbelievable and evolving at an incredible rate; fast forward almost two decades when the first PC was introduced, which made our lives even more productive, and with the advent of the Internet and cellular devices—wow!

Social media outlets are fun and do improve our way of life, but only as long as they are used responsibly, wisely, and in moderation. Abusing social media (being on there for hours at a time), texting endlessly, playing online games without being cognizant of time, to name a few, mindless and addictive activities are just like alcoholics and their addiction or our Welfare system being abused by people who shouldn't be on it, as a few examples which can be detrimental. Besides the typical issues associated with some teens (i.e., drug and alcohol abuse) below, I've summarized the top issues with many teens as they transition to adulthood.

	Top Issues Associated With Many of Our Teens
1	*Addicted to their smartphone* Excessive social media usage, texting profusely, app du jour, endless gaming, and talking to friends for hours at a time
2	*Lack of adulthood skills* • Self-discipline: goal management, time management, motivation, consistency, focus, accountability • Sound financial management practices • Career management • Relationship management: How to nurture key relationships
3	*Spoiled* For many, you still buy them a car and the latest smartphone. Actually, you will practically buy them anything to keep the peace and keep them occupied
4	*Spirituality is an afterthought* Good morals are not being practiced, and more teens are becoming atheists
5	*Educated on the Internet* There's lots of information on the Internet. Some good, some bad, and some downright ugly. Teens could use some guidance from you
6	*Not thinking strategically* They're living by the seat of their pants—not effectively planning ahead
7	*Lack of social skills* They spend so much time in their virtual world that many can't communicate effectively with people
8	*Living an unhealthy lifestyle* Not exercising or eating properly
9	*Causing tension at home* They're not always adhering to the priorities set by you. It's causing a breakdown of the family unit

10	*Not living with urgency* At this stage in their life, they think there's plenty of time: "what's the rush" attitude
11	*Not structured* They're not organized and don't follow an efficient routine
12	*Porn addiction* Several of my teenage clients and many adults are addicted to watching porn

The issues are astronomical and will only get worse as they get older and cause havoc for the rest of their life unless you help. I know you've got your hands full, and I will not sugarcoat the effort involved to mentor a teen just to sell a book. It's going to consume hundreds of hours as it did for me, but it will be the most rewarding goal in your lifetime. And if that's not challenging enough, most 18-year-olds have very little common sense or street smarts these days: once again, I attribute their lack of development to their addiction.

Common sense is nothing more than good sense and sound judgment in practical matters. My definition of common sense is to always think outside of the box, which means not always acting robotic or following a set of rules, i.e., do A, then B, then C. In many situations you have to improvise, react quickly, and make a decision that doesn't conform to what you've been trained to do. The best way to illustrate this is to use Alex's first driving experience as the perfect example. We all know that driving a car and reacting to situations on the road aren't always straightforward. You can't predict what the other person will do or when something unexpectedly happens, i.e., bad weather or perhaps a dog runs out on the road.

She did awesome acing the questions on her driver's permit exam and even took private lessons prior to getting her driver's license, but unfortunately on her first day out, she was driving me to the bank on her way to work. The speed limit was 45, and everything appeared normal except approximately 100 yards in front of us there was a logjam of about twenty cars. I took a quick gander and ignored her driving, *assuming* she would start slowing down as the cars ahead of her weren't going anywhere. I was enjoying the view from the passenger seat of my car, sitting there for the first time in years, when all of a sudden—bang, Alex just rear ended the car in front of us. She didn't slow down enough. The normal reaction would have been to take her foot off the gas and begin slowing down—not apply the brake 100 yards away, but certainly take her foot off the gas pedal and let the car slow down naturally, then apply pressure on the brake as the logjam of cars neared. Was it stupidity or just the lack of common sense? I would have to rule out stupidity.

The Real World

She was stuck in a time warp—in her virtual world (her fantasy bubble), oblivious to current events. It was disheartening, because supposedly she was an adult now, but she had no clue of what was going on with the real world: the economy, politics, and international issues. Here she was, continuously pontificating her adulthood status, but didn't keep abreast of current events, especially things that could impact her pocketbook. How can so many teens be so oblivious to what was going on in the world around them? Yet on the flip side they knew what was posted by their friends on Snapchat.

Adulthood Reality

There is a huge gap with young adults who are living at home versus being on their own. We've sheltered them way too much, and because their addiction has kept them occupied, we didn't have to put forth any effort to fix things until now. They need to feel some of the pain and pressures that you go through. In the Table below, I depicted a view of what adulthood could potentially look like for a teenager 10, 20 or 30 years from now.

19-22 Years old	• Attending college • Having a part-time job while living at home • Living in an apartment and working multiple jobs (e.g., movie theatre, restaurant, receptionist) to pay for rent, food, car expenses, utilities, etc.
23-29 Years old	• Retirement planning • If they're lucky enough to get hired by a good company, they will probably be working extra hours to prove themselves • Living alone or with a friend and paying high rent to live in a decent area • Car payments, maintenance bills, insurance premiums • If they didn't get a college degree, perhaps they're living in an apartment trying to find the appropriate job while working at a fast food restaurant • Saving up for a house • Marriage • Children • Daycare, food, piano lessons, baseball practice • Two cars to maintain, a home, credit card bills
30-39 Years old	• Same as above, but problems intensify year after year. Perhaps they have a second and third child and a bigger mortgage • Retirement planning

40-49 years old	• College for the kids • A larger home with an even bigger mortgage with bigger bills • Possibility of a divorce (50% chance in the U.S.), many go through severe depression due to custody battles over children, division of assets, and starting over again
50-59 years old	• Midlife crisis • Health problems and soaring medical bills • Difficulty recovering from professional/financial/personal setbacks
60+	• Count your blessings

These are all very likely scenarios!

And the costs associated with independent living are also eye-opening:

- Rent
- Car maintenance, insurance, and gas
- Food
- Clothes
- Entertainment
- Utilities
- Health and dental insurance
- Personal hygiene
- School costs (including books)
- Taxes. . .

The costs vary between states and cities. They will get the picture though. Below is the discussion I had with Alex to wake up and come over to the real world.

Real Life Scenario: The Real World (Current Events)

"Alex, do you know why it's so important to be aware of what's going on in the world?"

"Not really, I never pay attention to the news; it's depressing. I hate listening to all that negativity."

"I totally understand; no one likes negativity 24 hours a day, but unfortunately life is not so nice sometimes. Actually, it's not pretty half the time, and it will be that way for the rest of your life. Sh.. happens all the time, and there are incidents that occur and decisions that are made in the world, especially in Washington, D.C., that will affect your livelihood."

"I understand; I need to know what's going on around me."

"Yes, you do, it's important for you and your future family."

Although the discussion was good, I knew this was going nowhere; talking about it and doing something about it were as different as night and day.

"I need you to watch the news at 5:00 P.M. with me for the first fifteen minutes each day you're not working. Is that okay?"

"Okay, Daddy, for fifteen minutes."

Reluctantly she kept her word, and it actually worked—it was a real eye-opener. She had no idea what was going on in the world around her—incredible. However, she was making progress—asking a lot of questions, which was music to my ears.

A Note From the Author

Although publishers would categorize this book under the parenting genre, many adults grapple with these same issues, and my solutions apply for them as well. When I completed the original draft of this book, I passed it on to a few colleagues who are in the publishing business to critique my work. Their feedback was interesting:

- *It comes off like the author has a negative opinion about technology*
  On the contrary, I love technology. I actually grew up in Information Technology (IT). For the past four

decades it was my career as a Vice President in IT for a Fortune 500 multi-billion-dollar company.

- ○ I published over twenty IT Management related books with Prentice Hall under my own series titled *Harris Kern's Enterprise Computing Institute* (www.harriskern.com).
- ○ I love my smartphone. I am very dependent on it for my job as an IT consultant, speaker, and life coach (texting, FaceTime, voice and email) and in my personal life, I do my banking and manage my home with it (security, stereo, AC, and lighting). It is a huge time saver.

- *It comes off like the author has a personal tirade toward teens*
  Life is challenging, and time flies. You blink and you're ten years older, and nothing has been accomplished. I am trying to light a fire in our teens. Many display no sense of urgency.

- *It is heavily biased to the author's perspective and doesn't offer a balanced viewpoint*
  I highlight the most critical priorities: career, health, relationships, and finances. These are all top priorities, and I provide techniques on how to live a balanced lifestyle by focusing on these priorities. All of my solutions are real case studies from my life coaching engagements and my co-author's experiences as a teacher.

- *It sounds like the author has a personal agenda with his daughter*
  Yes, I do. She is the love of my life, and I want to see her succeed before I die. Wouldn't you want the same for your children? Her smartphone has inhibited her from progressing because she still resides in a virtual bubble. She wasted a good 6-8 hours a day on nonsense (yes, I am telling it like it is) on her smartphone. I will not sugarcoat the truth.

- *I personally see more adults hooked to a smartphone than teens*
  That may be true, but I wanted to appeal to parents to help our most valuable assets—our children. Starting from an early age, I wanted to place the emphasis on developing critical life skills and technology to be used as an enabler for success.

Smartphone use, just like anything else in moderation, is a good thing, but abusive utilization is not.

A Special Offer: Why Should You Buy This Book

I know there are numerous parenting books; however, the differences include:

- I will email you a *free copy* of my roadmap specifically designed to help transition adolescents to adulthood. I refer to it as the Personal and Professional Growth Program (P2GP). The P2GP is a proven process based on real-life scenarios from my life coaching business. It is designed to help teens break their addiction from virtual reality and promote the development of vital life skills. My email address is harris@harriskern.com
- The minimum set of adulthood skills with associated prescriptions to develop
- A simple and proven time management process for teens
- A simple and proven two-step process to help teens improve their self-discipline
- A proven methodology to help teens live with urgency and to hold themselves accountable

Sprinkled throughout the book are real-life scenarios (case studies) with teens whom I have mentored in my life coaching profession and also from managing my own daughter Alex's transition to adulthood.

SECTION I

The Strategy

I didn't need an adulthood strategy for my eldest daughter in the late 1980s (pre-cellular). The discussion was straightforward and brief: "If you're not going to college, you need to earn your own keep, beginning on your eighteenth birthday. Also, you will need to purchase a car when you turn sixteen, so start saving your babysitting and allowance money."

"Yes, sir," was my daughter's response.

I had that conversation right after her Bat-Mitzvah in 1991, when she was thirteen years old. I reminded her several times throughout her early teen years—just to make sure there were no surprises. She planned appropriately, focused on her priorities, and purchased a used car (on her own) when she turned sixteen. She had decided earlier that college wasn't for her, so she started working and eventually started her own business. I was extremely proud of her for planning and executing so masterfully.

Fast forward to 2016, when most teens are addicted to their smartphone and in the virtual playground they inhabit. They don't plan effectively and lack key life skills. Unfortunately, you are too busy to help them prepare, and besides, it's easier to buy them off with a car or the latest and greatest technology than try to take on that whole adulthood transformation quagmire. My situation with Alex was no different, but I wasn't about to buy her a car. I didn't do that for any of my other children, and she wasn't going to be the first.

I decided to get closely involved with Alex's transition to adulthood. I knew she was going to probably fail without my help, and in the end it would cost us both dearly. The first step with any large undertaking, i.e., a new business, a major project, or the most challenging venture of them all—helping our (new digital-age) addicted teens transition to adulthood. I needed a proven and well-tested strategy for Alex. Without a thorough plan, failure would be imminent.

The most important aspect of any plan is to get complete buy-in and commitment from participants—in this case, my daughter. It must also be simple to understand, easy to follow, and favor her dreams and aspirations. In other words, from Alex's perspective, "What's in it for me?" Below is a graphical depiction of my eight steps.

STRATEGY TO HELP TEENS BREAK
THEIR ADDICTION TO DIGITAL DEVICES

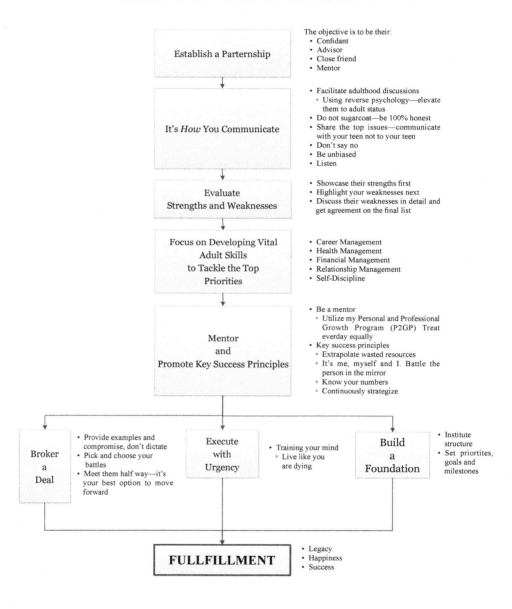

Establish a Parternship

The objective is to be their:
- Confidant
- Advisor
- Close friend
- Mentor

It's *How* You Communicate

- Facilitate adulthood discussions
  - Using reverse psychology—elevate them to adult status
- Do not sugarcoat—be 100% honest
- Share the top issues—communicate with your teen not to your teen
- Don't say no
- Be unbiased
- Listen

Evaluate Strengths and Weaknesses

- Showcase their strengths first
- Highlight your weaknesses next
- Discuss their weaknesses in detail and get agreement on the final list

Focus on Developing Vital Adult Skills to Tackle the Top Priorities

- Career Management
- Health Management
- Financial Management
- Relationship Management
- Self-Discipline

Mentor and Promote Key Success Principles

- Be a mentor
  - Utilize my Personal and Professional Growth Program (P2GP) Treat everday equally
- Key success principles
  - Extrapolate wasted resources
  - It's me, myself and I. Battle the person in the mirror
  - Know your numbers
  - Continuously strategize

Broker a Deal

- Provide examples and compromise, don't dictate
- Pick and choose your battles
- Meet them half way—it's your best option to move forward

Execute with Urgency

- Training your mind
  - Live like you are dying

Build a Foundation

- Institute structure
- Set priortites, goals and milestones

FULLFILLMENT

- Legacy
- Happiness
- Success

Chapter 1

The Eight Step Methodology

Utilizing the strategy above on Alex would be the true test. It took patience, tenacity, craftiness, and mega resources to help her develop the necessary skills to live a productive and happy life. Overcoming her deficiencies and helping her grow into a successful adult ended up being the most rewarding accomplishment of my life. Below are the specifics behind my proven 8-step methodology.

Establish a Partnership (1)

My objective was to be Alex's confidante, advisor, and close friend. I wanted to know everything that was going on in her life. I didn't want to be blindsided by something that could derail this endeavor. Her beauty, innocence, and awesome personality made her easy prey to a wolf who had the gift of gab and could penetrate her heart. I didn't want her doing something stupid like being with someone that would take advantage of that package. Perhaps even get her pregnant and destroy her future or catch some nasty STD. I wanted her to tell me everything, even the most personal things that she would typically only tell her closest girlfriends, and yes, that included the most intimate boy-related issues. We established a partnership, and she was proactively communicating with me at all times; we discussed everything together. How did I establish this sort of camaraderie?

Get Your Teen into His or Her Comfort Zone

If she's not comfortable, she won't open up. The most effective way to put your daughter at ease is begin having informal discussions about things that are important in her life, as painful as that may sound. This was no easy feat, because I couldn't stand listening to irrelevant babble about her friends, but I had to act like I cared. Whether it was about her school, boys, etc., I always portrayed the image of a mature friend who listened carefully and provided unbiased opinions. Also, don't always say *no* to most of her *wants* even if some of them sound ridiculous. Saying *yes* to the irrelevant ones will allow your opinion to be heard on the more important *wants*. It's vital not to belittle her ideas and goals no matter how ridiculous some may sound. To her they're all relevant, especially when she's discussing her future.

Once the comfort zone has been established, you should subtly and slowly introduce *reality* (without using the R word). It's your job to introduce and sell reality without trying to shove it down her throat. When she sees that you're on her side, then she will open up. She told me everything: how she experimented with cigarettes, when she wanted to get a tattoo, when she snuck her boyfriend into her room, and even when they cuddled in our media room, but she also told me nothing happened sexually, and if it did, she would tell me. She tells me when guys are hitting on her, when they ask her out, you name it, she tells me everything, and I offer advice.

Mentoring Alex was a painful ordeal because it took me away from what I love doing best: accomplishing major goals; but on the flip side, it's an awesome feeling having this sort of relationship with your teenage daughter. Below is a major discussion I had with Alex to help her decide whether or not to give her ex boyfriend a second chance. His actual nickname was Doofus. I labeled him Doofus because he was always doing dumb things, and it stuck with him. In the past Alex would have never included me in this type of relationship discussion, but since we developed our partnership, I was her primary source for personal and professional advice. Below was one of those delicate discussions.

Real Life Scenario: Becoming her Primary Source for Relationship Advice

They were only together for a few months, but she fell for him in a hard way. He was a bright guy, academically intelligent, very personable—had the gift of gab, a car fanatic, tall with good looks. Unfortunately, he had no common sense and was clueless on how to manage a relationship. He was harmless, but he was also very stupid, hence the Doofus label. About six months ago he dumped Alex, and that didn't sit well with me. I didn't like seeing my little girl cry for a few weeks. They were really a cute, wholesome couple. He was just young, immature, and clueless when it came to relationships. He didn't leave Alex hanging for another girl, it was due to a family dispute, and he had to quickly move out of his parents' home. He pretty much just walked out and moved in with a friend and his parents. He was going through major personal trauma and decided it was best to walk away from everything including Alex without saying a word.

Approximately six months later, Alex came into my office and said:

"Daddy, guess who sent me an Instagram request?"

"Who, dear?"

"Doofus. What should I do?"

"What do you want to do?"

"I don't know."

"I know how much you loved him, and I also think you still love him. Am I right?"

"Yes, you're right, Daddy."

When I first met Doofus, he grew on me over time, I felt he was a good kid, he just didn't have any guidance. His parents were wealthy and they spoiled Doofus; they actually bought him a brand new BMW when he was 16 years old. He had no clue how to manage his life or, for that matter a relationship, and here he was, almost 19 years old now. He could have easily taken Alex's virginity away from her because of his personality and gift of gab, but he didn't. I felt that he was just a kid whose parents pretty much left him alone and only provided financial support.

"Alex, God expects you to forgive, and that everyone deserves a second chance, but. . . you cannot be as accommodating and be there at his beck and call. You used to reply back to his text messages in seconds, if not minutes. That has to stop; he has to work hard and earn your heart back."

"I know you're right, Daddy."

"Listen, love, I hate to admit this, but relationships are a big game; if you don't play it well, you will lose. It's no different in the business world. Love alone does not solidify an association between two people; unfortunately, you have to manage your partner."

"But how do I play the game with Doofus?"

"It's simple; he wants you back and you want him back, but he's the one who ditched you. You have to make him chase you in a major way and do whatever it takes to win your trust again. Right now, you don't really trust him. If he walked out on you before, he will do it again unless you make him work hard for your unconditional love again, and then he'll think twice before ever doing that again."

"I understand."

"I will also tell you this about men. Make them work for your heart. If you make it easy for Doofus, he will get bored, but if you make it extremely challenging, then he will appreciate you that much more. Does all of this make sense?"

"Yes, it does, thank you, Daddy."

"You're welcome, but remember, don't reply to those text messages immediately like you used to do; play the game and play to win."

"I love you, Daddy."

"I love you, too, sweetheart."

It's *How* You Communicate (2)

One of the key success factors for this entire endeavor is your communication technique. My initial adulthood discussions with Alex were amicable, but they were going nowhere, as most teens think parents have an ulterior objective. Although she loved and respected me, I was still her dad. She wanted to do things her way and at her pace. I saw things differently, and her lack of development with critical life skills desperately needed a jumpstart. I had to equip her quickly, or society would swallow her up and spit her out.

The most effective way to proceed was to come down to her level and accept (for now) her current lifestyle, priorities, and goals. I had no choice but to treat her as an equal and take her input into consideration throughout this entire process. I couldn't bestow my disciplined mannerisms to life on Alex, because that would turn her off. It had to appear like this endeavor was her approach for happiness and success, which it was, but I knew what that meant and the effort involved to make that a reality and she didn't. It was important to move forward together and interject my wisdom in small dosages along the journey. All communication was played back in my head two or three times before speaking. I can't overemphasize the importance of communicating properly.

Below are tips on how to communicate with your teen. These are the same anecdotes I used on my daughter during her transition to adulthood:

- Treat her like an equal when speaking.
- Listen, do not dictate. Look at her facial reactions to sensitive issues. Make sure she's listening to you and the topic at hand. If not, stop and try a different approach.
- Produce solutions together. Work closely with her to help resolve difficult challenges.
- Be unbiased when making critical decisions. Look at her as a woman, not as your daughter.
- Reinforce the "family is a team" theme. Family minds are better than external influences. With family there are typically no hidden agendas.

- Do not sugarcoat the issues.
- Be honest and respectful.
- Spend quality time together. The further you bond, the more likely she will accept your advice.
- Compliment successes.
- Ask questions. Don't interrogate and don't press too hard.
- Don't make promises unless you plan on keeping them. They don't forget.
- Communicate frequently.
- If you have a teenage daughter like I do, who happens to be ultra-emotional during her menstrual cycle, try to avoid any sensitive discussions during this period.
- Always communicate in an even-keel demeanor. Never come off as moody. Being moody will put up a barrier that she will not want to cross. Always pay attention to the tone of your voice. Don't come off as unapproachable.
- Always encourage her to take on more adult-like responsibilities to help her mature, but do it in a very calculated and conservative manner. Don't move too fast.
- Ask for her recommendations to problems. Play role reversal constantly. Tell her to put herself in your shoes and make decisions. If you don't agree, negotiate an alternative solution together.
- Do not yell. Yelling doesn't serve any purpose.
- Don't pry and don't get too personal. Discuss sensitive matters at appropriate times. Tell her that you trust her and the decisions she makes.
- Have sensitive discussions while you are doing something together. For example, if you're cleaning the house—you don't want them to feel like you're putting her on the spot.
- Don't always do all the talking. Take turns; if possible, let her do most of the talking.
- Let her feel good about her worth. Alex happens to be good with technology; on many occasions I will ask for her help when I have an issue, although I can

probably find the solution. I make her feel like she's a big contributor to the success of my work and the household.

- Facilitate private times to discuss sensitive issues. We typically converse in the car, my office, or the media room, which is our favorite place in the house.
- Bring her into your world, albeit slowly. Share some of your thoughts and experiences. She also needs to understand the pressure you're under (i.e., paying bills and dealing with family issues). Let her feel some of your pain.
- If everything fails and there is a family crisis brewing with her, don't hesitate to get professional advice.
- Always communicate in the politically correct manner. However, if something she is doing or in most cases not doing that bothers you, then don't call her names, but address the problem. For example, Alex does a horrible job of cleaning her room, so instead of calling her a lazy slob, I explain to her that every part of the house is clean but her room. If that doesn't work, don't get angry, but let her know that if you have to clean her room, you would charge her for your time. That always worked for me.
- Don't judge, work as a team. You want her to share pertinent information, not clam up. It's we, not I. Sell her on the notion that two heads are better than one, but the final decision is always hers. For example, "We have an issue—right? We're both adults—right? Let's come up with a solution together. Two heads are always better than one."

Whew, that's quite a list. Like I said earlier in the chapter, it was much easier in the old days—a one-direction conversation. I would set the rules, and my eldest daughter would always comply. Despite the major challenges in raising a teen today, take a deep breath and enjoy it sometimes. Look at the positive side of any equation.

Assess Strengths and Weaknesses (3)

There was a huge discrepancy in skills required between Alex's goals and what's required to succeed as an adult. For Alex to accomplish her goals, she had to first grasp the depth of her weaknesses. I knew there were many, but it was important for Alex to visualize the long list of challenges she had to manage. In my life coaching profession I always started each engagement with an evaluation, which means I typically ask approximately 50-100 questions based on several different areas.

The competencies I assessed were:

1. Self-discipline
2. Leadership
3. EQ (communication, relationship management, etc.)

I also assessed:

- Drive and attitude
- Structure
- Health
- Finances
- Relationships

The competencies are used to determine the level and how extensive the mentoring ought to be in the future. She needed to understand her skill set rankings to actually grasp what she was actually capable of accomplishing at this juncture in her life. I initiated the evaluation by discussing her strengths. Don't lead with their flaws first. Your daughter will immediately tune you out. I actually repeated Alex's strengths a second time. I wanted to make sure she knew how proud I was of her accomplishments to date. Once Alex was feeling pretty good about herself, I shared my current and even previous weaknesses. I let her know that I wasn't perfect, and neither are most adults by a long shot. Below is the conversation I had with Alex the first time we discussed her weaknesses.

Real Life Scenario: Discussing My Daughter's Weaknesses

I was dreading the thought of having a discussion with Alex about her many weaknesses, but I had no choice. That evening she was sitting in my office discussing the typical nonsense— some friend-related issue, which reluctantly I had to show interest in and provide a recommendation; otherwise, it would be more difficult to begin the real discussion about her real-world challenges. After she thanked me, the real conversation began.

"Alex, do you know what my strengths and weaknesses are?

"I know some: you're smart, work hard, very successful, motivated, write a lot of books, and you exercise every day."

"Okay, good, not a bad start. Now do you know what my weaknesses are?"

She looked at me with a puzzled look and said, "I'm not sure.

"Do you know why you don't have an answer?"

"Why?"

I'm not perfect by any means, no one is, but my old mentor (yes, I had a mentor) and I had this same discussion over four decades ago, and I've corrected most of my weaknesses because I wanted to achieve self-mastery. To be successful, I had to accomplish my major goals quickly. I had many issues, but I attacked that list, and over the next few years I addressed my weaknesses. But enough about me, do you know what your weaknesses are?"

Without hesitation, she rambled them off (highlighted in the Table below). She did a good job of identifying many of them. I also chimed in and added a few more, which she agreed. It was important that we came to a mutual agreement.

Alex's Strengths	Alex's Weaknesses
Caring demeanor— has a big heart	Gets distracted easily
Academic intelligence	Addicted to her iPhone— even falls asleep with it in her hand every night. Text messages come in 24 hours a day
Good people skills— very personable	Very little common sense. On a scale of 1-10 where 10 equates to a high level of common sense, I would rate her a 1
Improved financial management practices: saves and is frugal	Immature
Maintains good morals	Lives an unhealthy lifestyle • Doesn't excersise • Eats many sweets
Dedicated and hard-working employee	Poor time management—a severe procrastinator
Punctual	Very low self-esteem
	Lacks confidence
	Poor memory due to constant distractions: texting and dealing with friends' issues
	No sense of urgency
	Wasting hours researching career options that are unrealistic

	Very emotional and temperamental during her menstrual cycle. It's difficult to have serious discussions when dealing with sensitive issues two weeks out of the month
	High level of drama with insignificant friend-related issues
	Confused about what she wants to do in life and is aggressively trying to prove herself as an adult but without a strategy
	Doesn't focus on adult-related priorities
	Unstructured: disorganized, can't follow a simple routine or create her own to-do list
	Doesn't keep commitments
	Doesn't think strategically

"Good job, Alex, now we can develop a plan to address these problems and move forward. How does that sound?"

"Yes, let's do it."

"I'm happy that you want to resolve your weaknesses; if not, I can guarantee you that these problems will not go away on their own with maturity. They just get worse, because the workload and family obligations will increase, and if you can't manage yourself effectively now—good luck in the future. If you're serious about fixing these issues, you will thrive; if not, you will struggle your entire life. It's always important to improve as a human being. Does all of this make sense?"

"Yes."

"Are you ready to fix those problems?"

"Yes, I am."

Once Alex saw her list of weaknesses, and I highly recommend that you show it to your daughter in writing, it will be easier to proceed. She was clueless as to the level of effort involved to fix these negative attributes. Begin by selling her on the most critical priorities for success discussed later in this book.

Develop Life Skills to Tackle the Top Priorities (4)

Academic skills are important, but without life skills your daughter will struggle or fail altogether. The priorities to ace as adults are: career, health, finances, and relationships. These are all critical to master, and in the next section I highlight the skills to develop for these priorities.

Mentor and Sell Success Principles (5)

Being a mentor to a teen is an important responsibility. In section III I discuss how to be their personal life coach. During the mentoring program one of your most important roles is to sell your teen on key principles that you believe will greatly impact their life.

These principles include:

- Treat every day equally
- Always know your numbers to effectively manage your life
- Continuously strategize
- Extrapolate wasted resources throughout the year. It's truly an eye-opening experience
- It's me, myself, and I. Battle the person in the mirror
- Learn to say no
- Live like you are dying
- Train your mind to hold yourself accountable

These principles are discussed in detail below.

Broker a Deal (6)

Try different methods until something actually clicks and promotes progress. I refer to it as brokering a deal. Brokering a deal means meeting your daughter halfway. Alex wanted to try things her way, which was understandable. I knew my approach was tested and proven; unfortunately I couldn't shove it down her throat, but I could convince her based on *what if* examples to understand the obstacles and the degree of difficulty with her approach. Even though she understood the pitfalls, the best I could do was meet her halfway. It was better than nothing, and once she felt some pain with her scenario, I was able to sell her on the proper path, which benefited her in a big way and significantly changed her decision-making approach on many different issues.

It's like being a fulltime politician and trying to meet halfway to get something done in our nation's capital. Meeting halfway actually works. Make it appear that her input is just as important as yours. Barking out orders and scaring teens only works on a select few. Brokering a deal always works. Below is a discussion Alex and I had before purchasing her first car.

Real Life Scenario: Buying Her First Car

This is the actual note I recorded on my computer. I then printed a copy and asked her to read it in front of me.

> *Dear Alex,*
> *Typically I would discuss these types of scenarios with you and try to broker some sort of deal to come up with one viable solution, but I felt that something as life-altering as buying your first car warrants a different approach. Although purchasing a vehicle may seem trivial to most teens, it's not. The responsibility of owning, maintaining, and driving a car is huge; therefore, I felt it's best to present the facts and let you choose from the three options below. By the way, as always, I am not going to sugarcoat any of my discussion points, and everything I write below is based solely on facts.*

The issues:

- *Our SUV is challenging for you to drive because of its size.*
- *You need a car to commute for school and work. Getting around in Texas is much more difficult than getting around in NYC, where you were born.*
- *Your friends have been driving for a few years now.*
- *You can't depend on Daddy to drive you around much longer because of his failing eyesight.*
- *The "I'm 18 years old now, Daddy" Syndrome.*
- *Purchasing a car includes paying for insurance, annual registration, maintenance (oil, tires, and brakes), gas, and future repairs.*
- *You currently have approximately $4K in the bank.*
- *You will need approximately $300.00 a month to maintain your car: insurance, gas, maintenance, registration, state certificate. This is barring any major car repairs, and when you buy a used car, there's always a risk involved; however, there are ways you can minimize the risk.*

The options:

1. *You can buy a clunker at any time for $2K and still have enough money left over to pay for insurance and maintenance, but it will be extremely risky and dangerous to drive, as it will probably break down frequently. Not something I would recommend for a young lady.*
2. *Buy a better car by yourself (perhaps spend $5-7K) at any time. Unfortunately, you will need to sign up for a loan, which would incur an interest charge on top of the loan payment. In my opinion, having interest charges is like flushing money down the toilet. Also, it's still an older car, which means it will be risky. Unfortunately, this is not any more viable than option #1.*
3. *Wait until you graduate from high school this year; focus on your grades (remember you are distracted easily). By that time you will have saved*

approximately $7K in the bank; I will loan you $2-
3K. Then you can buy a certified used car. You will
still have to repay your loan @ $200.00 a month
back to me, but at least it's interest-free and you will
get a better car, which reduces your overall risk.

"The choice is yours."
"I'll stick with option #3."
"Wise decision, sweetheart."
"Thank you, Daddy."

Tough Love

No two people are alike. Development in certain areas like common sense, self-discipline, EQ, etc. fluctuate based on family upbringing, peer influence, genes, mentoring, or lack thereof. Alex was lazy, unmotivated, and a severe procrastinator. She did her homework, but everything else was all about having fun and playing games on her smartphone. I've tried just about everything to light a fire under her butt—to no avail. My frustration came to a head—I had enough and went into the bowels of nastiness to share my thoughts. Below was my first conversation on laziness with my lovely daughter.

Real Life Scenario: Laziness Discussion #1

"Alex,
This isn't going to be pretty, but I have tried dozens of times diplomatically to put an end to your laziness, and nothing has worked. You and I have also discussed this subject many times, and we've tried implementing different solutions, including a simple morning routine that we both thought would work, but once again we were unsuccessful. Your laziness prevailed.

The routine was simple:
- *Get up one hour earlier—pop your head out of your room and say good morning*
- *Wash your face, get dressed, tidy room and the bathroom*

- *Eat breakfast*
- *Complete miscellaneous chores*
- *Brush your teeth and put on makeup*
- *Be out the door and in the car waiting for your dear old Daddy to chauffeur you to school or work*

This routine worked for approximately two weeks—then you always revert back—lounging in bed, being lazy, and foregoing your morning chores. This same scenario has repeated itself countless times. The most recent was this past Saturday; you didn't have to start work until 10:45. You got plenty of sleep, probably a good 10 hours, but instead of getting up at 9:45, you didn't get out of bed until approximately 10:05. Prior to this day, you were never late for work or school, but I knew that streak was about to end because I told you the night before that I required an extra ten minutes to do some banking before taking you to work. In typical Alex fashion, you lounged in bed until the last possible moment, and then you rushed around and didn't do your morning chores, and when we did leave, you jumped into the car without your socks, shoes, or makeup, which was all done in the car. You will not like what I'm about to say, but I am tired of discussing this topic. You keep telling me repeatedly that you're an 18-year-old, yet your behaviors depict a child who's maturity level is that of a 15-year-old. Besides your cutesy personality, great heart, caring demeanor, nice hair, and nice legs, what else is there? Ok, I'll concede you have a few positive attributes, but your list of negative characteristics is greater in magnitude and severity. It kills me to be reminded of these unflattering attributes. If you met some nice young man who had many of these attributes, would you want to be with him? I don't think so. You have great potential, but you're the laziest person I've ever known. You don't want to learn how to cook, can't clean properly, have no interests except your cellular, and you can't discuss current events with anyone. I guarantee you that the guys you date will get bored and move on. Is that what you want? Look in the mirror, the reflection may look good, but there's only superficial substance. Do you honestly think one day you're going to be marrying material unless you fix yourself now? Wake up, Alex.

Effective immediately, if you do not get up and do your chores, especially clean your room and bathroom, I will do it for you, but I will withdraw $50.00 directly out of your bank account. Any comments?"

"But you can't do that."

"As long as you live under this roof and not contribute to this household, I can do whatever it takes to get you to stop being lazy. Are you going to comply?"

"Yes, sir."

Did she change her ways? Not entirely, but she did improve enough to prevent loss of funds for a while. It was a very negative aspect of her life to break. A few months later, we had another brief discussion about her laziness, which is noted in the self-discipline section below.

Execute With Urgency (7)

Time flies. The next thing you know, you're fifty years old. You look back and ask yourself: "What have I accomplished?" Mentor your teen to not procrastinate when it comes to addressing their priorities every day. Below I discuss how you can train your daughter's mind so she will no longer procrastinate. She will be extremely focused on her priorities, goals, and milestones and nothing else. She will want to accomplish everything yesterday.

Build a Foundation (8)

It all starts with being structured. It is the foundation for success. Being structured means: following a to-do list, being organized, and following a routine. If your daughter can maintain structure she will be efficient.

This strategy is not rocket science, but it's not a quick fix either. It has gone thru several adaptations from being utilized on teens and adults in my life coaching business until it was ready for the grandest challenge of them all. Below is the first adult-related strategy discussion I had with Alex.

Real Life Scenario: Adulthood Strategy

You stood there glassy-eyed in my office doorway. It was Thursday 8/20/15' at approximately 9:45 p.m., you uttered the following words: "I hate this town, I hate my life, I hate my job, I want to attend a university somewhere else and not the community college here."

"Alex, we've had this discussion multiple times; it's not about where you live or where you go to school—it's about you. You need to fix Alex to be happy. You've lived in great cities: NYC, Los Angeles and you've traveled to many wonderful places as well: San Francisco, Lake Tahoe, Atlanta, Ft. Lauderdale, Orlando, Austin, Dallas, San Antonio, Houston, Athens, Paris, San Juan, and several other cities around the globe. Every city has two things in common: negative and positive attributes."

We live in a beautiful 5,000-square-foot home in a suburb of Dallas called Frisco, a wonderful town where the Dallas Cowboys have built their corporate headquarters and several NFL players actually live in our upscale, gated community.

I don't like seeing my little girl cry, but this was no ordinary weep session; besides, these emotional outbursts have been more frequent lately.

"What do you mean, I need to fix Alex?"

I remained quiet for a few seconds, then I said, "I will answer your question in a few days, sweetheart."

I decided to wait about a week until I was sure her menstrual cycle had subsided before responding. I had a two-week window every month to discuss highly sensitive issues. I actually marked it on my calendar in MS Outlook. Her emotions were sky-high during her menstrual cycle, and she didn't do a very good job of managing them. She knew it, and at times we laughed about it (post menstrual cycle), although for me it was no joking matter— it was torture. I actually walked around the house on my tiptoes. I always thought that Alex's temperament was impossible to cope with—actually was off the Richter scale during her period. I used to tell her, "I feel sorry for your future unsuspecting husband."

A few months ago, she was loving life with her hometown beau, who unexpectedly one day bailed on their relationship. Her emotions got the best of her, and that's when everything spiraled downward. The perfect bubble she occupied in the town she loved just burst. I had a bigger challenge to deal with, as Alex was not ready for adulthood—not even close. My dilemma was how to light a fire under her butt and prepare her for the realities of adulthood now. She was an emotional wreck; unfortunately, the luxury of time wasn't on her side. I needed to break through. I needed a strategy to help her get on the right path to excel as an adult, but it had to be perceived as her plan with buy-in and commitment, because eventually she would have to hold herself accountable. I maneuvered the discussion back to achieving her goals.

"It's important to know which goals are realistic based on your strengths and which skills we should develop to help you be successful. Is that okay?"

"Sure," she said with a cynical tone.

"Okay, now that we're on the same page, how do we address your weaknesses to improve your chances of completing all of your goals?"

She had a blank look on her face, which was predictable at this point in time of our discussion.

"Let me take a stab at this, but chime in if you think I'm going down the wrong path. Based on your goals, let's first establish the right set of priorities because to improve the odds of accomplishing your goals, you have to not only address your weaknesses, but also prioritize your life. Once we set priorities, then we can set realistic milestones for your goals."

"What does all that mean, Daddy?

"Let me simplify my lingo. I think one of your priorities should be to manage your finances. After all, you can't do anything without money, right?

"Yes, you're right, Daddy."

"It's much easier to be happy when you have money versus being in severe debt and miserable just trying to survive. Do you want to live for the rest of your life or just exist?"

"I want to live."

"Gee, I thought you would say that. Just so we're on the same page, effectively managing your finances means having a healthy savings account, knowing how much you spend at all times, never getting in credit card debt, and not constantly spending on the little stuff so you can eventually buy the big

things, which means you will enjoy a better lifestyle—right?"

"Yes, you're right, Daddy."

That was music to my ears.

"Before you leave my office, remember the hierarchy for success is setting priorities, goals, and then milestones for each goal?"

She looked at me as if I were a Martian.

"Don't worry, I will teach you all of that later, and it will make sense."

"Okay, good night, Daddy."

"Good night, sweetheart."

Two days later, when she didn't have any homework and wasn't working, we continued our discussion.

"We need to establish several financial goals. First, let's create a budget that will allow you to achieve your future desires. How does that sound?"

"Okay," she replied, although she had no clue what I was talking about.

"You need to constantly know your numbers so you can manage your finances, i.e., income, fixed monthly expenditures, unplanned expenses, and savings—right?"

"Yes," she murmured in a very soft voice.

"Let's establish another financial goal. You currently have approximately $4000.00 in the bank—right?"

"Yes."

"Since you would like to buy a car, perhaps the goal should be to have a balance of $10,000.00 in your savings account in one year's time. With $10K you can get a better car—a newer certified used car, how does that sound?"

She smiled and said, *"Cool."*

I could tell she was starting to get into this game called life, at least for now.

"We should also have a few rules and some guiding principles to live by—right?"

"What do you mean?"

"How about the following?

- *Don't spend frivolously on the little stuff, so you can buy the important stuff like a car and a home.*

- *Know your numbers at all times. Live by a budget.*
- *Don't get a credit card until you are disciplined enough to manage your finances, and always pay off your balance at the end of the month.*
- *Attend only one concert a year.*
- *All of your tip money should go into your savings account.*
- *No tattoos until you purchase a car and pay for your own insurance."*

"But I want to get my tattoos now."

Although I hate the thought of tattoos on Alex's body and spending money on this type of nonsense is irritating. I had bigger issues to worry about and just caved in to this "I want."

"Okay, you can have your tattoo."

"Yay."

I was building up Daddy points by playing along with the stupid stuff to eventually broker a deal on the more important things.

It was important that Alex leveraged my knowledge, love, and endless support to her benefit. Below is a discussion I had with her on how to use me—her best resource.

Real Life Scenario: Leverage Parents

Alex will need many allies to succeed as an adult. One of the worst mistakes young teens make is alienating themselves from their parents and trying to charge ahead on their own without proper planning and guidance. Although it's commendable, it's not a wise gesture. Alex tried, but quickly realized that her greatest ally is me, because I don't have any hidden agendas.

Below is the exact message I wrote for Alex titled, How to Keep Your Parents in Your Back Pocket, which I discussed with her in person.

"Alex,

First of all, congratulations on maintaining a 4.0 GPA after your first six weeks of your senior year in high school. You've done an incredible job, and I am extremely proud of you. You've also done a good job at work. That's the good news.

On the flip side, seven months prior to your graduation, you haven't developed intellectually to prepare yourself sufficiently for college. You've been unsuccessful with one university course (last year), and you've already failed many of your quizzes and exams with your second class. We agreed that without a degree, you will struggle for the rest of your life. It's not an option; it's a necessity in this era. You don't want to work in fast-food restaurants for the rest of your life. As an FYI, the average salary for a young adult who has a college degree (Bachelor's) is approximately $65K, and the person who only has a high school degree will earn approximately $31K: that's more than double. The competition for good jobs is fierce, and the ones who have the credentials have a better opportunity and will earn more money. I believe the root cause of the problem is laziness. I see a lazy daughter that's distracted by her friends and who hasn't grasped the seriousness of adulthood. You're not willing to invest the extra effort required to prepare for college, which includes hordes of extra reading. As far back as I can remember, you've hated to read. I used to always yell at you to focus while you attempted to read, but as I reflect back, it never helped, and now you're feeling the impact of not practicing effective reading techniques as you try to focus on college material. We both know your ultimate goal is to get a college degree; so how can I help you get there? You've always believed in the family unit and that we should always be together and be supportive of each other. Do you remember that phrase you used on us when we weren't always seeing eye to eye as a family?"

Yes, I said, "Way to be family."

"You made a good point, and you were 100% correct. It's all about the family and making sure that we help each other be successful. Although we are unique individuals with our own ideas, we have to work together to come up with one solution that we can agree on—especially you, because in the end it's your life. Currently you're not willing to invest extra resources to read your economics book. This has caused friction in the family, especially between you and Mommy, who loves you dearly. Due to your inadequate college AP course performance, we say no to just about everything that could distract you further.

Unfortunately we won't even let you buy a car with your own money, even though you have your license. We won't even let you drive our family car because it may distract you further by spending more time with your friends instead of studying."

Then you remind us, "I'm 18, I can buy my own car."

"Yes, you can, but you could potentially worsen your development efforts and alienate your family further. Is that what you really want to do? Remember we want the best for you; we don't have any hidden agendas like others may have. All we've ever asked of you is to focus on your education to date, and you deserve kudos for acing your high school courses, but now we have a major obstacle: Your laziness, lack of initiative, and no sense of urgency is preventing you from putting forth the extra effort required for your college curriculum."

"Alex, let's play role-reversal for a moment. If I were you, what would you tell me to do?"

"Daddy, I would tell you to try harder and focus on your studies."

"Okay, that's one thing I would say, but believe it or not, this is what I would say first: life is a bitch, but it's better than the alternative. You have the power to make it a good life; we all do. You're no different than me, everyone has the potential to be great, but how badly do you want to have that label? If you think someone is going to hand you a college degree on a silver platter or help you get that dream job, think again. Wake up and smell the roses, Alex! We love you dearly, but please wakeup."

"I know I get distracted, and I'm currently not college material, but what can I do?"

Then I blurted the following out, "Use me to help you succeed.

She looked at me weird-like and said, "Use you?"

"Listen carefully: most teens don't even bother communicating with their parents. You know how I operate, Alex, I am unbiased in my decision-making abilities. My recommendations are based solely on facts, and I always tell the truth, which is always the best policy. If I had someone with wisdom who I could use to discuss important issues, that would be awesome, but I don't. However, you do."

"I'm not exactly sure what you mean, Daddy."

"The word 'use' has a negative connotation with individuals outside the family, but inside our sphere it's referred to as help. I have a wealth of experience in so many areas; why not tap into it for ideas to help you make decisions? Life can be a real struggle; why not accept help from the most reliable source— your parents? There are no hidden agendas; all we care about is your success and happiness. Aren't two or three heads better than one?"

"That makes sense, Daddy."

"If I say no, ask me why. I'll tell you, I won't say, 'Because I said so.' I realize you're an adult now, and therefore you can make your own decisions. All I ask of you is to use me by listening to both sides of an issue.

"Okay, thanks, Daddy."

"Does all of that make sense?"

"Yes, it does."

"The bottom line is that I love you so much, I would do anything for you, and I've operated like that for your entire existence, but why stop there? If I was in your shoes, I would always want dear old dad on your side and saying yes. Once again, let me repeat: life is a bitch, and it wouldn't hurt to have my support. The only people you can trust to have your back for the rest of your life are your parents."

How Do You Know This Strategy Will Work on Your Teen?

The main purpose for writing this book is to arm parents with the strategy and tools to help their children succeed. It starts with a mindset change on your part to treat your teen as an equal and as a partner in their future. As mentioned previously, you need to make them feel comfortable to broker deals going forward. Below was a discussion I had with Alex. I title it the talk. What makes it unique is how I discuss life's most sensitive issues, not as a parent, but as her partner, without having to watch my P's and Q's.

Real Life Scenario: The Talk

Oh, how I dreaded having the formal birds and bees discussion with my daughter, but I was a single parent and I had waited long enough. It should have transpired years ago. Although, as a senior in high school, she's probably heard more than I could ever tell her, my chat was going to be different. It wasn't the same abstinence and STD talk that all teens hear, although I'll throw in some of that for good measure. My main concern with Alex was getting pregnant. I felt that any guy who had the gift of gab, charm, and loved a good hunt could infuse himself into her heart and take that coveted prize: her virginity. I know I sound crude, but I guarantee you that there are guys out there that are thinking in this manner, so why sugarcoat reality. She was also gullible; it wouldn't take much to win over her heart. Now don't read me the wrong way. She's not flirtatious or the partying type who hangs out with guys frequently. She is very selective, shy, and careful. She's an awesome girl, and being a virgin at 18 with her looks in this day and age is truly remarkable. Her values are showcased constantly—loud and clear, but it was time. . .

One day after we watched one of our favorite series in our media room, Sherlock on Netflix, I said, "Alex it's time for *that talk*."

She looked at me and smiled, "I knew this was coming, I just didn't know when, but I knew it was going to be soon."

"You've been progressing steadily, but I'm afraid something stupid could derail your progress. Do you know what that is?"

"I'm not exactly sure what you mean, Daddy."

"Look at yourself, Alex, you're a beautiful woman, and do you know what guys are seeing and smelling when you walk by? Let me answer that question: they see and smell fresh meat. They want what's in-between your legs, and many will say and do whatever to be the first. You won't have a chance, especially if he's good looking, has a nice personality, and can talk up a storm. If he steals your heart, takes your virginity, and gets you pregnant, you can kiss your future goodbye."

"Don't worry, Daddy, I am not stupid."

"I'm not saying you are: I'm just stating that some guys are sharks who smell fresh blood and will sneak up on you when

you least suspect it, and I mean that literally. Why am I saying this to you? Because I was the sneakiest and most cunning of all the great white sharks who loved fresh meat."

"You?"

"Yes, I went after virgins and I loved the sport. I can't begin to tell you how many unsuspecting young ladies I conquered and branded. Please don't take this the wrong way, I am not proud of my past sexual escapades, but there are others like me."

"Wow, you were like that?"

"Yes, the harder the challenge, the more I enjoyed the hunt until I got my prey. I could con any girl and any parent into thinking that I was an angel, while I was nailing their daughters and many of them in their own homes.

"Please be careful. I can't prevent you from having sex because in the end, you will do what you want when you're ready. Just please don't get pregnant and destroy your entire future. It's very promising right now."

"Thanks, Daddy."

"You're welcome; please be smart. And if you do have sex, please make sure you're thoroughly protected. STDs are plentiful out there."

"I promise to be super careful, Daddy."

I smiled and said, "I love you, Alex."

"I love you, too, Daddy."

SECTION II

Developing Vital Adulthood Skills

Life 101 wasn't taught in high school, and it won't be taught in college either. Unfortunately, your son won't be taught the most important skills from his academic curriculum.

The skills I am referring to will help him address the following issues:

- How will he plan for a rewarding career?
- How will he manage his finances?
- How will he excel in his current job?
- How will he maintain a good health regimen?
- How will he nurture important relationships?
- How will he motivate himself every day of the year?
- How will he hold himself accountable?
- How will he focus on his goals?
- How will he live life with urgency?
- How will he remain consistent?

If you're wondering whether or not your son can learn these skills on his own, the short answer is yes; heck, the answers to many of these questions can be found on the Internet, but unfortunately, there is just as much bad information as there is good. How will he know what is useful? He won't, because the Internet is only a good resource to supplement your wisdom; otherwise, there is just too much stuff out there to research.

Where to Begin

The most important skills to teach your teen fall under the categories of finances, career, health, relationships, and self-discipline.

- *Finances*
  Managing the basics: spending, saving, investing, and budgeting. Below I have documented my ten principles for sound financial management practices.
- *Career*
  How to interview, schmooze key people, get that promotion, and other tips on how to grow in your career. Also understanding the importance of the 3-Ps (performance, perception, and politics).
- *Health*
  Teens are extremely vain; heck, so are most adults, but Alex breaks the vainness scale. Below I've highlighted a few tips on how to use that to your advantage and sell your son on the importance of taking care of his body by maintaining a good health regimen. The body and mind work most effectively as one. Exercising consistently and managing his eating habits will keep him healthy and productive and grow his confidence.
- *Relationships*
  God, family, business colleagues, and friends. Making time to nurture key relationships is typically put on the back burner when the pressures of everyday life consume all available resources. Below are a few tips on how your son should maintain relationships.
- *Self-Discipline*
  The #1 problem is procrastination, but that's only the tip of the iceberg. Overall time management is poor,

and scarce resources are taken for granted. Failed goals, being unmotivated, no sense of urgency, lack of focus, and inconsistency are areas that will cause havoc for your son if you don't help him address these issues now.

There are many important skills to teach your son to help him build a successful and happy life, but it's crucial you teach him the most vital ones. Learning makes life interesting, fun, and challenging. Below is a story I shared with Alex about always growing her knowledge base.

Real Life Scenario: Continuously Seeking Knowledge

"Alex,
Learn from everything and everyone around you, not just from your friends, the Internet, and formal education. I'm referring to those everyday experiences and challenges we all face. Whether it comes from traveling (cultures, languages, etc.), understanding your body's physical limitations, or completing a huge project at work, keep on learning. Even in my elder years I love to learn; it's one of the things that makes life so rewarding. I'd like to share this story with you, which I have titled the continuous thirst for knowledge."
"Okay, Daddy."
"I was on assignment in Washington, D.C., the birthplace of politics (being somewhat facetious). Politics is the most dreadful business-related term (in my opinion) in the dictionary. Oh, how I hate that word—always have, until recently. I felt that politics was for people who couldn't accomplish anything, and politicians were spineless weasels (as you can tell, I have a very negative opinion on this topic)."
"Wow, I had no idea you felt that way."
"I was facilitating a week-long strategy workshop at a very large and profitable corporation in the D.C. area. The first day was miserable. My frustration level was at an all-time high. In attendance were Vice Presidents and Directors. By the end of the first day, it was apparent that very little

would be accomplished because of all the hidden political agendas in this company. I was ready to burst. Up until then, my presumption had blocked me from seeing any usefulness in the political system. However, I found out from one of the VPs during a coffee break that financial targets are met even if it is in their own bureaucratic and entangled way. I started to see that even in the midst of all these agendas, things could get done. Unbelievably, by the middle of the second day, I wanted to learn how they did it. I had become curious. Something that I had felt so strongly against was now something I wanted to learn about. I had an incredible thirst to understand how politics could be used to someone's advantage and how to weave in and out of agendas to accomplish an objective; and by the end of the week, it made sense. With politics, especially the D.C. type—you learn not to fight it, but work within the system. Do you understand my point, Alex?"

"Yes, that makes sense, Daddy."

"I hated politics so much that I shut it off until I learned how to take advantage of it to help my career and eventually make a lot more money. If you get a corporate job, I will teach you how to play the political game and use it to your advantage. Every company has some sort of politics imbedded in its culture."

"Okay, I will listen and learn."

Chapter 2

The Ten Principles to Effective Financial Management

Most teens don't know how to manage their finances, and that included Alex. She didn't understand the basics of effective money management. It doesn't start and stop by getting a paycheck and depositing it into your checking account. It's how you manage your finances that counts (pun intended), and most people do not make financial management a priority and undoubtedly get into a bind. The ten principles below are proven, genuine, and simple to follow. I've used them for over four decades to transform myself into a multimillionaire at the age of 38 and also to help hundreds of life coaching clients (including teens) manage their finances and investments wisely.

Make Finances a Priority (1)

Does this mean you need to tell your son to think about money around the clock? Yes. I am not going to beat around the bush. When finances are a priority, he will have peace of mind. It doesn't necessarily mean he will be happy. That is a separate issue altogether, but without money life for your son will be a continuous nightmare.

Making finances a priority means he should:
- Maintain a budget
- Think twice or three times before making any purchase, always questioning himself before handing over that credit card to the clerk
- Know his numbers at all times
  - How much is in his checking account
  - How much is in his savings account and having enough to tie him over for at least one year, in case he was unexpectedly laid off
  - How much is he earning
  - How much is he spending
- Continuously trying to beat his numbers
  - Beat the balance in his savings account consistently. Grow, baby, grow should be his motto
- Train his mind to be frugal and make every penny count
- Have multiple sources of income
- Stop spending on the little stuff to buy the important things
- Establish financial goals, but set milestones to ensure success

This is a good start. If he accomplishes these activities and follows these principles, he will achieve financial security. Below is one of the first Daddy/daughter discussions I had with Alex, and it wasn't about the birds and the bees.

Real Life Scenario: Money IS a Priority

"Alex, do you know that managing your finances wisely is vital for living a happy and successful life?"

She replied back with one of the most silliest phrases in the English language, "Money can't buy you happiness, Daddy."

"Yes, you're right, sweetheart, but without it you will be unhappy all the time. You can forget about going to concerts, and moving out with your friends will be nothing but a fantasy. Unfortunately, it's the way the world operates—it revolves

around money. It isn't everything, but it's a necessity. Without the proper resources, turmoil follows; it's probably the number one killer for most marriages. Did you know that?"

"No, I didn't know that."

"Without money you are going to be one miserable little puppy; forget about buying your favorite car one day, a Porsche, and traveling the world. Effectively managing your money should be a top priority along with your health, education, career, and relationships. Don't think of money as the root of all evil, as so many claim. Money is wicked only if you let it destroy your morals and forgo your values."

"Aaah, I guess you're right, Daddy, it's really important."

Her first part-time job was babysitting: she was so excited after getting paid $20.00. Initially she wanted to spend it, like most teens, but I convinced her to open up a savings account and deposit her funds. Right from the get go, I said, "Alex, don't spend your hard-earned income on nonsense. You will need it to buy a car. Trust me, it all adds up."

"But, Daddy, I want to buy some really cool earrings and hang out with my friends at the mall."

"I understand; perhaps there's an alternative solution. It appears you'll be babysitting for our neighbors frequently; each time you do, deposit 50% of your income into your savings account and keep the other half. When you save enough for those earrings, then buy them. How does that sound?"

"Okay, that's fair."

"Who doesn't want to spend money all the time, sweetheart? Unfortunately life doesn't work that way; you will need every dollar you earn. Use it wisely to pay bills, to live, for emergencies, to buy the luxurious stuff, and also to have some fun. It's all doable; you just have to manage your money."

"I understand."

"Remember, you have to buy your own car eventually; I won't buy one for you."

"I know, I remember."

"Good girl."

Alex's friends spent money like there's no tomorrow because their parents didn't teach them how to manage their finances, mainly because they never made financial management a priority. Many of them didn't have any savings, were in debt, and would spend more than they made, just like our government. Don't let this happen to your son.

Train Your Mind to be Frugal (2)

The most effective way to help your son be frugal is teach him how to train his mind. Just asking him to manage expenses prudently does not work.

Below are techniques he can use to permanently change his spending habits:

- *Establish negative phrases that promote an image of going broke*
  "In case I lose my job, do I have enough money in my account to support my family for at least one year?"
  Or he can go one step further and use hardcore negative phrases like: "I am going to lose my job any day, and I won't be able to support my family."
  This was my favorite phrase, I preferred hardcore phrases. It helped me save more by withdrawing additional funds from my paycheck and depositing them directly into my savings account, which meant I had less disposable cash each week for expenditures.

  Some may argue that the odds of losing your job are minimal, especially if you get your job done immediately and maintain a good relationship with management. They may also argue that being this negative would cause you to be so stressed out and depressed that you could lose focus on getting the job done in an efficient manner. I was laid off twice in my prestigious and long IT career—it was a harrowing experience. It had nothing to do with my performance. It had everything to do with the economy. After my first layoff, I wanted to make sure that if it happened again, I had a huge savings account, and that's the reason I went hardcore negative. Not saying IF but WHEN, and guess what it happened again? Being negative internally did not change my disposition, but it made me work harder, smarter, and more efficiently.

Have your son create his own phrases. If he prefers to use positive affirmations, have him establish phrases that promote an image of being successful by having a hefty account and savings as much as he can any time he can. If he trains his mind effectively, he will be frugal. He will also question every purchase and be very selective about making that purchase.

- *Value all monies*
  Even coins. You worked hard for it. Think twice or three times before walking over that coin—pick it up and put it in that big coin jar at home.

- *Don't view minor expenses as a one-time occurrence and that it's no big deal*
  Wrong, it is a big deal as it all adds up. Extrapolate all expenditures throughout the year, and it will be a shocking experience. I would always tell Alex, "Be frugal—save for the big stuff." The more she would spend on the little stuff (i.e. Slurpees from 7-11, candy bars, sodas and knickknacks from the mall), the less she had to make those significant purchases. That $10.00 she spends each week on nonsense adds up over the long haul. That's $520.00 a year ($10.00 x 52 weeks) flushed down the toilet on incidentals, and sometimes it's more than $10.00.

- *Being frugal doesn't mean you can't have fun*
  Alex and I go out to dinner at least once a week. We don't spend much; a typical bill averages $20.00, which includes tips—we don't purchase beverages. I taught her to avoid ordering drinks from restaurants because that's where most establishments make their profits. The $5.00+ we save on sodas or coffee each week will net us a few hundred dollars at the end of the year, which will allow us to dine out more frequently. If she feels like drinking a soda, we always

have a 2-liter bottle of Sprite (her favorite) at home, which we bought on sale at WalMart for $1.00.

- *Even if you're rich, don't flaunt it; guess who's watching*
  We own 5 homes outright (no mortgages), Alex knows we're wealthy, but I don't spoil her nor do I showcase our lifestyle. Teach your son at a very young age to treat money judiciously. I work out at 24-hour Fitness, and I'm always spotting coins around machines and picking them up. Every year I roll up those coins (while Alex is watching) and deposit it into my savings account—approximately $50.00 annually. Alex gets tips from work daily, typically a few dollars. All coins and bills go into a jar; at the end of the month she rolls up those coins and deposits it into her bank account. That's my girl!

- *Being frugal with utilities—it's a preventable waste*
  Utilities can be a huge expense if you look at it as a necessary evil and not manage it. I taught Alex to look at it as a preventable waste. Being mindful of utility costs goes a long way in saving money. I save hundreds every month compared to my neighbor who has the same size home, but doesn't manage his utilities. Below are a few simple methods you can teach your son on how to reduce his utility bills:

  ○ *Water*
    - When he takes a shower, teach him to: wet himself down, turn the water off, lather up, and then turn the water back on and rinse off. He should not leave the shower on the entire time. The same goes when washing his hands. Wet them, turn the water off, lather up, and clean them thoroughly and then rinse.
    - He should not flush after going to the bathroom each time he urinates unless of course you have company; otherwise, pee at least 3 times before flushing.

- Make sure he fills up the washing machine each time he washes clothes. He should never run the washer and dryer with only a few items.
- He should never leave the water on while washing dishes. Rinse them first, then turn the water off. Soap them down and then turn the water back on and rinse.

- *Electricity*
  - Make sure he always turns the lights off after leaving a room.
  - Teach him to remove half the bulbs from lighting fixtures unless it's the family library or reading room from his own place. We have a large home. Each room has a reduced number of bulbs. This saves us plenty on our electricity bill each month.
  - He should use energy saving bulbs.
  - We have a beautiful pool in our primary residence. If I listened to the pool cleaners and builders, they would have me run the pool pump for eight hours a day; I run it for 4 hours a day in the summertime and only 2 hours a day in the wintertime, which is sufficient. I've been doing this for over two decades, and my pools are fine. I've saved thousands of dollars over the years and continue to save on my electricity bill. Once again, I am saving on the small stuff.
  - He shouldn't constantly open the refrigerator door or leave it open for a prolonged period of time.
  - He should turn off the television when not watching.
  - He should always buy energy-efficient appliances.

- *Gas*
  - He shouldn't have the heater running 24-7 in the winter (wear more layers of clothing).

- They say you should set the heater at 68 in the wintertime. I set it at 65, and everyone wears an extra layer of clothing.

Taking frugal to the next level

Grocery bills are difficult to swallow when you're a young adult living on your own and trying to make your miniscule income stretch to pay bills. Every week, sale items would be advertised on a flyer from our local grocery store. I would let Alex pick out the items we need, and we would go shopping together. I could easily spend twice as much if I wasn't watching for sale items.

Below are some additional tips on being frugal you should discuss with your son:

- *Car*
  - Buy a car that's fuel-efficient and reliable.
  - Never rest your foot on the brake pedal or clutch while driving—not only does it put unnecessary wear and tear on your brake and clutch, but it also wastes gas.
  - You shouldn't carry unwanted weight in your car—the heavier your car is, the more gas you waste.
  - Maintain your car on a regular basis—have your oil changed every 3,000 miles.
  - Rotate the tires regularly—if at all possible, you should rotate them every time you change the oil.
  - Change the air filter frequently. A dirty air filter can waste gas.
  - Tires should be inflated properly. It saves a considerable amount of gas.
  - Observe speed limits. It saves gas and prevents you from getting speeding tickets, which are quite costly.
  - Avoid unnecessary stopping and braking.
  - Accelerate slowly and smoothly—this saves a lot of gas.
  - Wash your car at home. You won't throw away

your hard-earned money at a car wash. Besides, it's a good form of exercise.

- *Social*
  - When socializing with friends, don't show off by frequently picking up the tab at a bar or restaurant.
  - Don't go to evening movies—attend matinees— you will save half on your tickets.

- *Cooking*
  - If you cook a casserole or lasagna, make enough for several days. This saves time and money on your utility bills.
  - Make sandwiches and snacks and bring them along when taking a long car ride or when you're waiting at the airport for a flight. Airport food is quite costly.
  - Plan and cook your meals based on the deals you get from the grocery stores (look religiously through the weekly sales flyer).
  - Cook more meals at home.
  - Bring your lunch to work frequently. Avoid going out to lunch regularly.
  - Make your own coffee—stay away from gourmet coffee shops.

- *Home*
  - Eliminate unused magazine subscriptions.
  - If possible, relocate to an area with a cheaper cost of living.
  - Use Skype for long-distance video calls.
  - Review your cell phone charges—remove services that aren't being used.
  - Don't own a pet when you first move out. You will save money on food and veterinary expenses.

- *Insurance*
  - Pay your car insurance semi-annually or annually. Insurance companies charge more if

you pay monthly or quarterly.

- ◦ Do some research before filing an insurance claim. You shouldn't submit a claim unless it's at least twice the amount of the deductible. If your deductible is $500.00, do not submit a claim unless it's substantially more than $1000.00. Typically, insurance companies will raise their rates after one incident—but you may want to check with your agent to find out what the impact on your overall bill will be.

- **Credit**
  - ◦ Never leave your credit card numbers active with online accounts—it's easy to forget about them, and a subscription you may not necessarily want to renew will have already renewed itself automatically year after year.
  - ◦ Get a credit card that offers you reward points—but does not charge you an annual fee.
  - ◦ Improve your credit score. You can save hundreds or thousands of dollars on interest when purchasing a home or car.
  - ◦ Pay off the balance of your credit card each month. Do NOT incur new debt. You should use your credit card for all purchases if you get airline points or cash back.

- **Computing**
  - ◦ Don't leave your computer on when not in use.
  - ◦ Turn off the power on your printer when not in use.

- **Banking**
  - ◦ Never do business with a bank that charges bank fees (e.g., checking account fees). Find a more customer-friendly bank that offers free checking and no maintenance or finance charges.
  - ◦ Avoid ATM fees. Only withdraw cash from machines approved by your bank.

- *Shopping*
  - Avoid impulse buying. Plan ahead every time you spend.
  - Limit gift-giving.
  - Make a list when you go shopping and always make sure that you stick to it.
  - Many name-brand shampoos are expensive—add water to your shampoo to get more uses.
  - Shop at discount stores like DSW, Target, Ross, and T.J. Maxx.
  - Buy generic medicines.
  - Don't go to malls or shopping centers for entertainment.
  - When purchasing a major item, use cash as a negotiating tool. All vendors' eyes light up when they see cash.
  - Buy items in bulk when they're on sale—especially products that don't spoil.
  - Buy generic brand products at your favorite grocery store or from other well-known and popular stores (e.g., Kroger, WalMart, Target).
  - Do not purchase magazines or newspapers. Read them online or go to the library.
  - Book flights in advance.
  - Use ebates, a free online coupon website. You can get cash back when making purchases.
  - When purchasing items offering rebates, make sure you keep your receipts and submit the rebate form.

- *Health*
  - Don't smoke, drink alcohol, or do drugs.
  - Cancel unused health club memberships.
  - Cut back or eliminate altogether fast foods or microwaveable convenience meals.
  - If you take daily medication, instead of getting a monthly refill, you should ask your doctor for at least a three-month supply.
  - Consistently exercise and manage your eating:

you will remain healthier and save on medical expenses.

- *Miscellaneous*
    ◦ If you sign up for a new service which has signup fees, ask them to waive it. Eighty percent of the time, they will.
    ◦ If you live close by to a library, go there. Utilize their free services (e.g., Internet, DVDs, movies, magazines, social opportunities).
    ◦ Don't spend money to de-stress; find alternative methods. Going on an expensive vacation each time you feel too much pressure is not the answer. The debt you incur will outweigh the 1-2 weeks of temporary relief.
    ◦ Get DVDs from Redbox for $1.50 per rental.

The bottom line is that there are plenty of places he can save, and if he trains his mind, he can make that happen consistently. Below is a discussion I had with Alex about being frugal.

Real Life Scenario: Extrapolating Income and Expenses

Alex and her girlfriend would hang out at Starbucks and have a cup of coffee at least once a week. She would also purchase a cup of coffee each morning, much to my chagrin; that type of expense can add up quickly. One night we were discussing finances, and she was complaining about her expenses, and I mentioned Starbucks. Below is the conversation we had.

"I love Starbucks, too, and I would love to drink a few cups of their coffee every day (morning and afternoon). You know I can afford it, but I don't."

"What's the harm of spending a few bucks a week? I make pretty good money. I need to live, Daddy."

"I don't go in there because I won't spend $2.00-$4.00 for a cup of coffee—that's ridiculous; if I do that twice a day I would be flushing over a hundred dollars a month down the toilet.

That's more than $1000.00 a year on just coffee."

"Ouch, I never thought about it like that before."

"You're probably spending between $100.00 and $150.00 dollars a month there. Next time, extrapolate the amount you spend in one week over a year's time, and I bet the sticker shock will force you to reduce your visits or stop altogether."

"OMG, Daddy, double ouch!"

"You can get a cup of coffee for a buck in many places; it may not be as good as Starbucks, but some are comparable, and the difference in your pocketbook will make it taste that much better."

"You're right, Daddy, I will find somewhere else to hangout, cut it back to once a week, or stop going altogether."

Now she only goes once a week and orders one cup of coffee—her treat for the week. Teach your son how to train his mind to be frugal by extrapolating all expenditures. Alex worked as a cashier at a fast food restaurant, and they pooled tips; the cashiers were responsible for dividing the proceeds at the end of their shift. If she forgot her share of the tips, it would be split between the rest of the staff. She would forget at least twice a week. I used to get so frustrated. *One evening I mentioned, "Look at tips as income over a year's period. Let's say you average $1.50 a night in tips. Don't look at it as $1.50. Extrapolate that amount times 20 business days X 12 months, and you have approximately $360.00 in tips for the year. In every scenario whether it's income or an expense, extrapolate the amount over a year's time—it works."* She no longer forgets her tips.

Have Multiple Sources of Income (3)

The bills will always be there, but your son's current job may not. He should never be satisfied with one source of income in case one dries up. In this Internet business-conducive era, it's easier to have a side business or a second job. Teach him never to be complacent and constantly strategize for opportunities.

Maintain a Budget—Always Know Your Numbers (4)

If your son doesn't know how much he spends, then how can he manage his resources effectively? This situation is not rare. Many of my adult coaching clients are unaware of how much money they spend. Then they seek my services because they're in severe debt and can't pay their bills. Unfortunately, by then it's a major challenge to rectify. Help your son establish a formal budget. If he's computer savvy (and most teens are), help him create a simple spreadsheet that highlights his income and expenses. He probably doesn't know what a budget is—teach him that it's a summary of intended and expected expenses for a certain period of time. Take the time to sit down with him and observe his income for the period. Now list absolute necessities, those expenses he has to pay in order to live: rent, food, transportation, utilities, vitamins, medications, etc. Always include savings as part of his basic expenses. Then list his bills. There are his monthly bills, such as credit cards, rent, and utilities, and then there are other ones. Which ones need to get paid? If he has little to work with and has to choose which bill to pay, think carefully of the consequences of not paying that bill. Now have him list the things he would like to purchase if the income demand is met. These are desirables (i.e., dinner out, a new purse, etc.). He needs to know the balance in his checking and savings accounts at all times. If he doesn't know his numbers, he can't manage his finances effectively.

Save and Beat Your Previous Number (5)

Begin teaching your son to save all of his allowance and other income as soon as he starts earning money. Savings must be a priority. I taught Alex to consistently save and never withdraw funds from her savings account, unless it's for a major purchase like a car or home. It should not be used for vacations or Christmas gift shopping, it should only be used for major necessities and investments. He should set an amount and deposit those funds into his savings account each time he is paid. Even if it's a very small amount—he needs to just do it. If he deposits funds consistently and watches his number grow, his mind will be trained. It will always want to see more—to always beat his previous number. He needs to be obsessed about saving money.

Invest in Property and Your Company's 401K Program (6)

Purchasing a home is still one of the best and safest investments despite the collapse of the U.S. housing market in 2008. Teach your son to continuously save for that ultimate purchase—a home, but only entertain its feasibility if he has enough resources to make those monthly mortgage payments on time and he can establish an emergency fund (savings account) to pay his mortgage payments for at least one year in case he loses his job. Investing in property has always been a wise move, and if he can sign up for his company's 401K program, it would also be a smart, sound, and safe investment. Make sure he doesn't rely on our government for his retirement. Property typically appreciates, and 401K programs are an excellent way to invest, especially for his elder years.

Be Risk-Averse (7)

Your son shouldn't invest in the stock market to make a quick buck. In 2008 the market lost 35% of its value. Millions of people will never recoup their losses. If he takes the time to learn how the stock market works and looks at it as a long-term investment, then it's probably a good thing. Also teach him not to get involved with any 'get-rich-quick' schemes. If it sounds too good to be true, then it probably is!

Don't Lend Money to Friends

Your son should never lend money to associates or friends. He will probably never see his money again, and his friendship will deteriorate or potentially end. He's worked hard to earn that money; you have a duty to mentor him so he will protect those precious resources.

Debt is a Nasty Four Letter Word (8)

Teach your son to avoid credit card debt at all costs. He should never buy something if he can't pay for it in cash. The best way to ensure he complies is to not only discuss the horror stories associated with credit card debt, but consider starting the learning process in a very controlled manner. Get him his own credit card *under your account* and tell him to bring a receipt for every purchase, and you will deduct the amount from his checking account. Make sure that he understands that if he abuses the use of the card, you will cancel it. Scaring him does work, and taking small steps forward works, too. I used this approach on Alex, and it worked like a charm.

Credit cards are only good if you're teens are disciplined

If your son possesses financial discipline, then credit cards are a good thing because many cards have rewards (airline mileage, bonus cash, etc.) based on usage. If he always pays off his balance at the end of the month, then it's a very good thing to earn those rewards. They also help him establish credit history, which is critical when it's time to make that big purchase. If he has poor financial discipline, it could be disastrous, because most cards carry high interest charges when carrying over a balance to the next month. Discourage him from getting his own credit card at first unless he truly is disciplined. Explain to him the horror stories of credit card debt spiraling out of control and the millions of people who have to file for bankruptcy because they couldn't manage their finances. He needs to hear those horror stories.

Tough Financial Love is Healthy (9)

Although you may feel sorry for your son and want to keep buying him things like clothes and amenities, begin weaning him off of life support and let him start earning his own keep. Alex needed to start feeling some adult pain. The same sting I felt each time I paid the bills. She really had no clue; it was time to get her toes, then her feet wet. It's called tough love, but it's really not that tough, because I was still paying for that roof over her head, meals, and utilities. I started very slowly by making her pay for clothes and amenities. Cut the cord with your son as quickly as possible. I did it with all of my children. As much as I loved them, they needed to figure out how to make it on their own. I told them they wouldn't have to pay rent or their share of the utilities as long they went to college. It hurts, but I couldn't show it—it's the only way. I also didn't buy any of them a car. They got that message loud and clear on many occasions throughout their teen years.

Communicate About Money Early and Often (10)

Talk about money, how your son earns it, invests it, and how he plans to spend it. You shouldn't be afraid to comment on the good and bad financial practices of other families, as well as on ethical issues. And when he asks questions, answer him in an age-appropriate fashion. Avoiding the subject of money can make it seem dirty or shameful.

Most of you would never let your son get behind the wheel of a car without taking lessons, getting some practice, and earning a driver's license. Yet these days you might send him off to college or live on his own without the necessary money skills.

Chapter 3

Health Management

Their addiction: playing video games for hours or watching a few dozen videos on YouTube contributes to an unhealthy lifestyle. In many instances they're too tired to exercise or take the time to eat properly. Portray a healthy lifestyle for your son. If you do it, there's a good chance he may see the benefits as well, but if you're lazy and unmotivated to exercise, what do you think may happen to him?

Maintaining a good health regimen is a must. Even with this well-known fact, it was difficult to sell the importance of making health a priority in Alex's life. I had numerous conversations with her until I finally broke through, but it took trickery to seal the deal. Not only did she loathe the thought of any sort of activity, except tiring her fingers out from texting several hours a day, but the thought of sweating wasn't very appealing. Although I exercised seven days a week, her mom exercised consistently, and even her grandmother exercised a few days a week; with all that inspiration and dedication you would think she might get motivated, too, but it had zero influence. She was lazy and proud of it. Forcing this issue wasn't working, her mother and grandmother would always ask her to go and exercise, and the answer was always no. A few weeks went by, and I decided to take a different approach. I attacked her where I felt the greatest impact would be—her appearance. We all know how vain teens can be about their looks—she was no different. Although she had a fairly nice body, standing 5'5" tall and weighing 130 pounds, she had a decent package, but she wasn't happy with it because she had no hips and her butt wasn't round enough. One day we were spending some quality time in the pool. After a few hours we got out to dry off, and I decided to go for the jugular. Below is the discussion we had that got her to start exercising consistently.

Real Life Scenario: She Hated Exercise, Now Loves it

"Alex,
If you want to fit into that bikini like a model, you need to do something about it in the gym."

"I know, but you know I won't go to the gym—forget about it, besides I'm in perfect health, why should I exercise? I hate it, and I think sweating is disgusting,"

"Do you think I like exercising every day, sweetheart? I can think of many different things to do and at the top of the list would be to sit on the couch with the remote in my hand watching movies."

"Why don't you, Daddy?"

"Because exercising is where my energy and stamina come from, but we've been through all of this before. Let's discuss this further later."

I remained silent and decided to write her an email later that evening after she went to sleep—below is what I wrote:

Alex,

Only I would tell you this sweetheart . . .

This afternoon I said you had no hips, a mediocre butt, and your shoulders are too big—this is reality. You're uncomfortable with your bottom half—always covering it up. Although you have awesome legs and many other beautiful physical attributes, the fact that you have no hips and a butt that's not round enough bothers you. I am not going to sugarcoat the effort it would take to build an hour-glass shape—it will take hard work, time, and dedication—also my time to train you.

Below is what it will take to reshape your body:
- *Do heavy squates to widen and round your butt further. Doing 4-5 sets and 10-12 repetitions per set using some poundage.*
- *Do lightweight shoulder exercises to cut some of the fat off. Do exercises of 20 reps for each set. This is a total cut-up and reshape routine.*
- *Do arms with very light weights and lots of reps—20 per set—not to bulk but to cut up.*
- *Do wideback/lat exercises with medium weight to widen out your upper back—so you won't be straight from top down.*

That summarizes some of the exercises you will need to do for your body, but you also have to train your mind to maintain consistency. Be truthful, look in the mirror, is that the body you want? Do you always want to cover it up?

It's up to you.

Love you,
Daddy

After this email I never said another word about her body. In a few weeks she approached me and asked if she could go to the gym—this was music to my ears, and she's been going consistently ever since. I taught her how to train her mind to hold herself accountable. For additional information on how to train your mind to hold yourself accountable, read the book titled *Going From Undisciplined to Self-Mastery: Five Simple Steps to Get You There*.

Below are some exercising tips you should consider teaching your son:

- *Exercise daily—it's the only way to maintain consistency*
  You don't have to go to a gym every day; you can take a nice brisk walk or wash the car or clean your room or apartment. Unfortunately, the only way to be consistent is to train your mind to make it part of your daily routine. Working out a few days a week rarely works over the long haul (although there are exceptions), but in most cases, it becomes one or two days a week and then missing an entire week. That's because your mind gets used to taking days off, and it will always want to do that, but if you train your mind by exercising every day, exercise becomes habitual and becomes part of your daily routine.

- *Constantly change your routine*
  I change my routine weekly. If you don't change your routine frequently, your body will not make the proper gains. Also, the odds of you getting bored increase considerably.

- *Constantly challenge yourself*
  It's fun to beat your previous best—right? What a feeling! For example, if you burn 315 calories on the elliptical machine on Monday night, you should try and outperform that number the next time you get on that machine. You may not always beat your number, but it's motivating and keeps things interesting.

- *Exercise in the morning*
  Exercise wakes up your metabolism. How long does it take for you to be alert when you arrive at work? A few cups of coffee? How much productivity is wasted each day because you're still sleepy? Thirty minutes? An hour? How many hours for the week? How many days are wasted throughout the year? When you exercise before you begin work, you're already alert when you get to the office. The wheels in your brain are already turning at a high RPM for hours. Additional benefits include:

  - *Having a positive outlook all day long*
    You will feel great. Your demeanor will be positive. There's no better way to start the day!

  - *Improves the quality of your sleep*
    You will definitely sleep better at night. If you had problems sleeping previously—waking up earlier to exercise should remedy that. You should also have less problems falling asleep.

  - *You're more creative and resourceful*
    You will be more creative when you're well rested, stimulated, and energized.

  - *Your productivity will increase*
    It's easier to remain consistent when you make exercise your first major activity of the day. With consistent exercise comes a higher level of energy and stamina; therefore, productivity will increase.

  - *Regulates your appetite for the rest of the day*
    You will eat less because since activity causes the release of endorphins, which diminish your appetite. Another bonus is that you will eat healthier foods.

○ *Increases mental acuity*
Studies have shown that exercising significantly increases mental acuity—a benefit that lasts four-to-ten hours. Exercising before going to work means utilizing that extra brainpower when it's mostly needed—not wasting it while you're sleeping because you worked out in the evening.

Below are a few helpful tips to teach your son on how to manage his eating habits:

• *Don't eat too much*
Easier said than done; however, it's quite simple to manage: if you indulge one day, you need to cut back the next day, but don't waste precious cycles by measuring calories for every meal unless you have nothing better to do with your time. Everyone knows when they eat too much and especially if they eat the wrong things. It's like anything else in life; you need to do things in moderation.

• *Manage carbohydrates*
Eat fewer carbohydrates in the afternoon, early evening, and definitely before going to bed. It's all about strict maintenance of your carbohydrate intake (breads, pasta, potatoes, and rice), as well as portion control (total number of calories consumed). You need to learn to manage the urges of your body.

Exercising consistently and managing your eating habits should be a way of life. If it's not on your son's radar now, it will be later, but not by choice.

Chapter 4

Career Management

Alex did a good job of finding part-time work, but that was the easy part. I never coached her to look at the big picture: How to research career options, prepare for an interview, communicate with management, strategize for that promotion, and thrive utilizing the 3-Ps (Performance, Perception, and Politics). If your son is lucky enough to get hired by a large company, he should understand how the corporate world operates. Guidance on how to navigate through a pack of wolves could be the difference between success and failure.

Get closely involved and help him develop the skills to head down the right path. Sure, it's his career choice, but there's a huge difference between choosing a career, securing it, and excelling in it. This is an area he wouldn't know how to prepare for diligently; it wasn't taught in school. If he makes the wrong decisions along the way, it could be difficult to overcome. Good jobs aren't that easy to obtain, and mistakes could be very serious and could take a long time to correct; besides, guess who may have to support him in the long run if he fails?

Strategize Career Options

All teens should continuously strategize to be more efficient and successful in every aspect of their life, especially in their career. If your son is lucky enough to land a good job with plenty of opportunities for growth, he should always put pressure on himself to grow and never be complacent. Wether it's looking for faster ways to complete a project or how to get that coveted promotion, especially during what I refer to as dead zone times like commuting to work, being in a meeting that's politically motivated and has no real value, or waiting for his doctor appointment.

Below are some career-related areas for your son to strategize:

- What is the next move he should make?
- Which position can he get promoted into that will give him more power and a bigger pay check?
- Who is his greatest competition, and how does he eliminate them?
- What new skills does he need to master for advancement?
- Which skills does he need to secure a management position?

The gears in his head should always be spinning at a high RPM and strategizing. Come rain, sleet, or snow, he should always plan for that next career move, reviewing organization performance or trying to think of ways to implement a key project faster and under budget. If your son wants that rare position, he's got to outsmart and outperform others. He needs to be proactive and look for things to do, whether it's in his department or another. He should never wait to be told what to do. In any large organization that is growing quickly, there are always initiatives that could be undertaken to improve the efficiency and morale. His goal should be to outperform his previous best and try to outperform others as well. This will help him get on management's radar and stay there. Out of sight, out of mind is the best way to describe not being on management's radar. Below is one of the first career-related discussions I had with Alex.

Real Life Scenario: Career Discussion

Alex used this phrase dozens of times: *"Daddy, I don't know exactly what I want to do in my life yet, but I want a job that makes me happy to get up and go to work every day, plus it will allow me to travel the world."*

She spent many hours researching career possibilities. I didn't have the heart to burst her bubble, but I had to introduce a major dose of reality before she continued to spin her wheels looking for the perfect job that would make her happy and fulfill her financial needs.

"Alex, everyone wants the perfect job; who wouldn't want to look forward to getting up in the morning and going to work? It's an awesome feeling, and it's great that you're taking this so seriously. May I make a few suggestions?"

"Yes, of course, Daddy."

"You should consider having short-term and long-term career objectives."

"What does that mean?"

"Sorry, sweetheart, let me elaborate. You should have several options, because unfortunately, career decisions are not solely yours to make. You're dependent on others, i.e., the hiring manager, Human Resources, and other company employees who would have to select you over other potentially qualified candidates."

"Aren't you being negative, Daddy—what happened to all the encouragement?"

"I'm not being negative or trying to discourage you, sweetheart. I'm merely stating a fact and being a realist, but I'm not telling you to stop or slow down your ambitious process—on the contrary, I just want you to be well prepared for the hiring process and for potential rejections. There are no guarantees when you're dependent on others."

"Okay, I understand."

I knew that her chances of landing a dream job in the short term were very slim, but I couldn't say that; I needed to work around her naiveté. My role was to persuade her to look at other job opportunities without bursting her enthusiasm and not letting her think this was just something I wanted versus what she wanted to do in life.

"Long-term, you should continue looking at those jobs that truly excite you. Jobs that entail travel and utilize your photography skills. You may also expand that search to include other jobs that pay well (just in case your primary choices don't pan out), so you can still earn enough to travel the world on your own. Does this make sense?"

"Yes, it does."

"You should also pursue jobs that are more recession-proof and pay well, like healthcare. Perhaps learning to be a physical therapist. You enjoy helping people, and this type of job is always in demand. It also pays well, and you'll earn a good income so you can travel on your own terms."

"I'm not crazy about working in the medical field and being around all of that pain and suffering."

"I understand, sweetheart, but try and look at careers with more of an open mind. Remember what you always tell me— don't be so negative—right? What if you traveled to different military facilities helping soldiers overcome their injuries and seeing a smile on their face from performing a movement they couldn't do before, now wouldn't that be cool?"

"Yes, that would be exciting," she said as her head was bobbing up and down.

"There are many different career options; don't limit yourself, just in case your first choice doesn't pan out. You will still need to earn a living. One other field to consider in the short-term is to try and leverage that award-winning smile and that awesome personality to apply for an entry-level position in a large business or company. Then if you're lucky enough to get hired, try working yourself up through the ranks, at least until you find your dream job. What do you think?"

"Okay, sounds good, Daddy, this really helps me a lot. Thank you."

"You're welcome, love."

"Remember, when you're fresh out of school with no real experience, you need to be a little less selective. You know how extremely picky you are about your clothes, food, hair, etc.; well, you need to change your decision-making parameters

*when it comes to your career. When it comes to your hair and
clothes, it's all about you. When it comes to getting a job, it's
about you and your potential employer. Does that make sense?"*

"Yes, it does."

*"It's important to start building your resume. You've worked
in two fast-food establishments, and even though you've been
a great employee, it still isn't much of a track record. This is
reality, sweetheart."*

*"I understand, thank you, Daddy. This conversation helped
me a lot. I won't be as picky; I really need to develop my
credentials."*

"That's the way to look at it, love."

The Job Interview

It all starts with the interview. The competition is plentiful
and fierce; the better your teen is prepared for that stressful
interview, the better his chances of landing the job.

Below are some tips on how your son should prepare and
conduct himself for a job interview.

- *Research the company thoroughly before the big day*
  Understand the services they provide and their
  corporate structure and try to memorize their vision
  and mission statement (if available on their website).

- *Dress appropriately*
  It's important for him to always dress nicely for
  an interview. It also shows that he's serious about
  getting hired for the position and respectful of the
  interview process.

- *Be polite, courteous, and personable*
  He should not be dry and boring, but also not come
  off as immature, corny, and unprofessional.

- *Practice for that interview*
  Prepare him thoroughly by asking a few typical
  interview questions like what are his strengths and
  weaknesses. Why should somebody hire you. . .

- *What not to ask*
  What does this company do? Can I change my schedule if I get this job? If I get this job, when can I get time off for vacation?

- *Have a resume*
  Don't let him go to the interview empty handed. If he doesn't have a resume, help him create one. There are plenty of sample resumes to choose from on the Internet.

- *Watch a job interview video*
  The more prepared he is, the better. If he's never been through a formal interview, I highly recommend that he watch a job interview video. He'll find several on the Internet.

- *Be honest*
  Make sure he never bullshits—a good interviewer will know it.

- *Be confident*
  The interviewer knows that your son is not a seasoned veteran—he's not going to have much experience, if any. When he speaks to the interview team, tell him to portray confidence in his abilities.

- *Be energetic*
  Tell him to display passion in his voice and showcase his energy. Make sure he doesn't slouch or appear laid back—he must always come off as being energetic.

- *Make eye contact*
  Teach him to stay focused on the interviewer. He must not get distracted.

- *Thank the interviewer*
  When the interview is complete, make sure he thanks the interviewer for their time and that he hopes to hear from them again.

- *Thank you note*
  Make sure he sends a thank you note to everyone he interviewed with. He needs to let them know that he's still very interested in filling their job listing.

- *Key things to get across in the interview*
  Even if he's not asked certain questions, make sure that he showcases his structure (organized, follow a to-do list, etc.). During the interview it's important to let the interviewer know that he can manage himself efficiently.

It's important for the interviewer to feel like your son is engaged in the meeting and that he's not only done his homework on the company and the position by answering the questions to the best of his ability, but he's also asking questions throughout the interview. Asking questions shows that he's interested in the position, and just as important, it opens up a two-way dialogue. The more he communicates and, therefore, bonds with the interviewer, the better his chances of reaching the next level in the hiring process. It's important for him to make a connection with the interviewer.

Below are a few questions your son may consider asking the interviewer:

- Is there opportunity for growth and advancement in this position?
- Is this a newly created position?
- Who are the key people I will be interacting with?
- What are your expectations for this position for the first 30-90 days?
- How would you define success for this position?
- What do you like about working here?
- How would you describe a typical day/week in this position?
- Who does this position report to?

Ask questions about the company like:

- What's the company culture and management style like?

- Is there a corporate strategy for the next 3-5 years?
- I didn't see a mission statement on the website; is there one?

As the meeting concludes, make sure he asks the interviewer what the next steps in the hiring process are. Remember, your son is in competition for that one position with other talented people; the more he prepares, the better his odds of landing that job. Below is a conversation I had with Alex when she unexpectedly asked me to take her to a job interview after school one day.

Real Life Scenario: Her First Job Interview

"Daddy, can you drive me to a job interview at the mall after school today?"

"Sure, sweetheart."

I knew she had been seeking part-time employment, but she wanted to surprise me with the interview. As we were driving there, she said, "This is my first job interview."

I was assuming that she was already prepared. I dropped her off at the mall and said, "Good luck, sweetheart."

"Thanks, Daddy," She seemed very confident.

I found a spot under a tree in the parking lot to read while I was waiting for her to finish. I figured I had at least one hour. I also figured that this was a slam-dunk, because she mentioned that one of her friends who worked there referred her to the hiring manager.

Within 10 minutes she came out, and I immediately asked, "What happened, I was just getting comfortable under this tree?"

"It was horrible, I don't think I got the job."

"Didn't you prepare?"

"Not really."

"Sweetheart, it doesn't work that way; just because a friend of yours referred you doesn't mean the interviewer will hire you."

The next few weeks I spent time facilitating mock job interviews to prepare her for the next interview. She was really clueless on how to prepare and conduct herself in a formal interview. I'm assuming most teens are in the same boat. Two weeks later, she had another job interview and was hired on the spot.

The First Thirty Days

Your son has to make his mark quickly, because he's on the radar. He has to be resourceful and do whatever it takes to learn his job and get it done in a quality and timely manner. Learning his new job responsibilities and determining whether or not he will be liked by his peers and management will be very stressful. Most companies are not going to give the new kid on the block a long time to learn his job, and he probably will not have someone shadowing him for a few weeks. If he's lucky, he may get a few days of classroom training and a few manuals to review with very little on-the-job training time.

Teach him to establish the appropriate perception immediately—like the first day, by staying past the time he's supposed to get off and always get in early, preferably prior to management arriving on day two. Tell him to come in as early as possible even if he doesn't get paid for it. He needs to show management that he's a company person from the get-go.

The first 30 days in a new job is critical for overcoming any skepticism that's institutionalized in most companies for all new hires, which is why it's important to minimize any uncertainty as quickly as possible.

Below are a few tips to teach your son to ensure a great first impression:

- *Be friendly and personable*
  Approach people in the break room, say hi—introduce yourself. This is the best way for him to learn how the department operates.

- *Learn departmental values and corporate culture*
  He needs to fit in quickly.

- *Be respectful and courteous to everyone*
  Self-explanatory.

- *Join coworkers for lunch or coffee*
  Even if he doesn't have the time—he should do it.

He needs to get acclimated to the team as quickly as possible.

- *Ask questions*
  He needs to ask his coworkers for advice on the dos and don'ts for his first 30 days. Also about dress code, culture, how meetings are conducted, and who the key players are.

- *Take plenty of notes*
  More importantly, make sure people are seeing him take notes, but not take notes on his phone during these first 30 days.

- *Make it a point to meet with management regularly*
  Especially in the first week, but he needs to come prepared with an agenda. Discuss training progress, 30-day plan, status reporting, and management's expectations.

- *Be extra diligent not to make a mistake, but if he does, he needs to admit it immediately*
  Let management know and also tell them what he will do differently next time.

- *Don't make waves*
  It's better to keep quiet during the first few weeks and listen and learn.

- *Change email settings to engage spell-check and a one-minute send delay*
  Email is a great productivity tool, but it could also be his worst nightmare. If he's not sure how to articulate an important message—he needs to draft something, save it, and check it the next morning when he's not brain tired before sending.

- *Don't step on anyone's toes*
  He may find things in the department that could be performed more efficiently; if that's the case, he needs to approach management and start each sentence in this manner:

- ◦ "This procedure works well, and I'm just the new employee here and still learning, but I was wondering if you've already tried to do. . . "

- ◦ "I am sure this has been tried before, but I was thinking, what if. . ."

- ◦ "You guys have been doing this a lot longer than me, but here is a thought. . ."

It's crucial to sell your son on the importance of developing a 30-day plan to help him succeed in his new job—right out of the gate.

The 3-Ps

It was Alex's first real job (post fast-food restaurants and babysitting): a company with approximately 150 employees in the suburbs of Dallas. Although she was hired on as a receptionist/administrator, there was tremendous opportunity for growth, especially with her hard work ethics, smile, and personality; but without the proper business skills she was going nowhere. I needed to prepare her quickly, and I needed to minimize the number of skills and simplify the learning curve. I placed them into three categories: Performance, Perception, and Politics. I refer to these as the 3-Ps for success.

Performance

Superior performance is a direct result of continuously strategizing, prioritizing, being efficient, focusing, maintaining structure, managing goals, being resourceful, and operating with a sense of urgency. Possessing these characteristics means that your son is disciplined. It's also important for your son to demonstrate that he is a company person. This means working diligently and investing extra hours in the evenings and on the weekends. He should be prepared to invest many hours if necessary. Sometimes it will be unavoidable. But other times he may be able to outsmart management by making it appear that he's working more hours than he actually is—aka the perception game.

Perception

Let's say your son would typically work fifty-hour weeks. If he follows these simple steps, it will appear to management that he's working sixty to seventy-hour weeks when he's not. In the corporate world perception is a key success factor. He shouldn't think of it as being deceitful. Consider it more like battlefield tactics to outmaneuver or outsmart the enemy. He should do it in a method where it looks like he's investing more hours than he actually is. Let's say it's Wednesday, and his project is due the following Monday. He should do as much as possible Monday— Friday, and even if he finishes his project Friday afternoon, he shouldn't email the deliverable just yet—wait until the weekend. Every manager looks at the time stamp on emails that come in during off-hours. Work-related emails he sends during these off hours will draw management's attention. They will typically recognize him as a company person. They will believe that he's thinking about his job day and night and he's doing whatever it takes to get the job done.

Following this simple piece of advice will help his career immensely. Congratulations, your son has just won a strategic battle. It's also a good idea for him to work an extra few hours to catch up in a quiet environment. Early Saturday morning, perhaps before his family or significant other wakes up is ideal. Your son should send an email to management and his team throughout the weekend. Once again, the perception is he's been working around the clock. But in reality he's not, and that goes a long way.

Politics

Perception and politics are very closely linked. Other things he can do to make a good impression and get ahead is outmaneuver management and fight back in the politically correct manner, especially when interacting with management during the week about a certain project that has been assigned to him with unrealistic demands. As much as he may want to, he shouldn't say no—he should tell management that he will work on it over the weekend and send the deliverable before Monday. He should remind management (subtly) that his current customer-related responsibilities will fill up the work week, and he doesn't want to drop the ball on anything. He shouldn't make it look like he's complaining. It's just a gentle reminder that his plate is full, and he will get to this very important project over the weekend when it's easier to complete the work without interruption. He should work on the project and complete as much as possible during the week, as time permits, but not tell his boss and click send sometime over the weekend. Your son needs to be subtle with his actions, making sure management knows over casual conversations that he's worked over the entire weekend.

The same advice goes for status emails. He should complete them and place each one in his Draft Email folder—then click send in the evening. It looks like he was working around the clock, but he's actually not. If he wants to be noticed, he should have a plan before just doing it. One more thing: he shouldn't communicate directly with management. Do it indirectly. For instance, if someone asks how his weekend was, he should consider responding this way, *"It was excellent. I had fun with my family and accomplished a great deal on my work project, too."*

It's a well-known fact that approximately 90 percent of all the world's assets belong to a small group of people, which is comprised of one percent of the earth's population. Many individuals will do just about anything to excel in their career to be associated with this elite group. That included me. To achieve this level of success, it was important to play the *"political game"* well. To excel in my career, I had to compete in this highly difficult and competitive sport. Yes, I refer to it as a sport because the competition is fierce, and there's always a clear-cut winner and loser. It's a high stakes game! Working effectively (including thriving in politics) and being ultra productive will typically get you a nice bonus and perhaps a promotion.

To survive and thrive in the business world, your son has to be shrewd and observant and have the gift of gab, just like politicians. Whether he works in the private or public sector, the larger the company, the greater the political atmosphere he will have to endure. Having to embrace the political landscape of any company seems like such a complete waste of time, but to be successful, he either plays the game and does it well or simply moves aside so he won't get trampled by those who are in the game to win. It's that simple!

Develop Professional Relationships

If you don't teach your son how to *proactively* manage professional relationships, his success in the corporate world will be limited. Schmoozing with the right people will help him get ahead. Typically, nurturing key business relationships is taken for granted and put on the back burner, which is a huge mistake. Promotions and bonuses are not only based on performance, perception, and how well you play the political game, but, sadly, on who you know. I would constantly say to Alex: *"If you focus on professional relationships, it will improve your earning power."* Get right to the point—don't sugarcoat this fact of life. Your son needs to pick and choose relationships with key executives who can enhance his career.

Tell your son that he needs to locate the key stakeholders who can eventually help him get that promotion. Once located, he needs to schmooze with the people that will help launch his career. Schmoozing is how he should network. It also plays a big role in marketing and sales, getting deals done, developing and maintaining long-term relationships with customers, and garnering support from peers and coworkers.

My wife struggled in her management career because she failed to schmooze with the appropriate people. As she put it, "I'm not about to kiss anyone's butt."

I replied: "Schmoozing was not about kissing someone's butt. In fact, the definition of schmooze is to converse informally, to chat, or to chat in a friendly and persuasive manner especially so as to gain favor, business or connections."

Below are ten tips you can teach your son to help him build strong relationships and business connections through the art of schmoozing:

1. *Don't BS*
   BSing destroys credibility. If he wants to become a successful executive or leader, he shouldn't BS. It

doesn't matter how smart others think he is, just how smart he really is.

2. *It should never be about him—it's always about them*
   Connecting with people means finding things he has in common with them or even different views on a subject they both feel strongly about.

3. *People like to be schmoozed*
   People like attention, to be noticed, to connect and engage. That is, as long as he's straightforward about it.

4. *Be open and genuine*
   He needs to be himself. The most effective way to connect with people and find common ground is to be himself, with all his native charm, faults, and idiosyncrasies.

5. *Don't overdo it*
   Next to BSing and trying to be someone he isn't, *trying too hard* is the biggest schmoozing pitfall. Pushing too hard will backfire.

6. *Everyone is schmoozable*
   CEOs, VPs, tough administrative assistants: everyone is schmoozable, for the simple reason that everyone likes the attention—under the right conditions.

7. *Always be appropriate*
   He should never overstep his boundaries or make others feel uncomfortable. He should never invade someone's personal space if he's not sure what the limitations are. It's different for everyone, so he needs to pay attention; they'll let you know.

8. *Always be respectful of people's time*
   Now more than ever, time is our most precious resource.

9. *Don't talk at people*
   Nobody likes to be talked *at*. They like to be engaged. They like to be listened to. There's a big difference. Just remember: give a little, get a little.

10. Let yourself be schmoozed
> Although, by definition, schmoozing is related to persuasion, he'll be better off just thinking of it in terms of long-term relationships. That means he should always be willing to help people first. It's good karma.

That's quite a long laundry list. Without practicing these pertinent skills, his career could stall or even worse. . .

Chapter 5

Managing Personal Relationships

Your son's resources will become more scarce as he matures and takes on more adult-related responsibilities. Once he completes his daily milestones and obligations, there will be very little time left over. Then there are his family obligations—that should get top billing—right? The first step is to realize that he needs to pick and choose relationships most critical for success and happiness.

I recommend building solid relationships with:

- God
- His girlfriend or wife
- A *few* close friends

Once he crosses the adolescence/adult threshold, reality commences, and the number of friends (real or virtual) that he currently spends dozens of hours with each week will slowly diminish, but it's important to remain close to a *few* good friends. We all need a *few* close friends.

Proactively Manage Your Partner

As hinted to above, your son's plate will be full. There will always be more activities on his plate than hours in a day. If he has a partner (wife, girlfriend, other), it's important that he's proactively managing his relationship. Negative situations in relationships can stop anyone's productivity. Your son is no exception. It could bring him down for days and weeks; it's the number one killer to productivity. We have entered into relationships since the Stone Age. What we have not been able to accomplish yet is to maintain healthy strong relationships. What exactly is a strong relationship? One in which two people work together toward a common goal. It is not abusive in any manner. It is communicating and coming to a common compromise; there are no winners because you worked together. So what does it take to build that strong relationship?

Below are some helpful tips to teach your son:

- *Trust*
  Trust is everything. Without trust there will be no relationship. He can have a shell of a relationship, but nothing will truly be there. Think about all the people he knows that question their partners about every little detail of the day. Trust is vital for any relationship to become strong and everlasting.

- *Honesty*
  Where does a relationship go without honesty? No one truly wants a relationship based on lies. Even white lies will eventually turn into great big lies that forever need to be covered up. He needs to be honest with his partner at all costs. Lies are like a poisonous gas that will silently kill any relationship.

- *Spend time together*
  Sounds easy, right? Think again. With the hustle and bustle all around him, it is extremely hard to make time for anyone in his life. Sometimes he will have a tendency to forget that the other person is there. Once again, tell him to be proactive and spend some quality time with his partner.

- *Forgiveness*
Forgiveness is essential for a strong relationship. Now, I am not saying to forgive unfaithfulness, but he can forgive his mate's harsh or offensive words every now and then. Sometimes we get into moods and say things we really don't mean. As long as this doesn't happen daily or even weekly, he should take the time to find it in his heart to forgive his mate.

- *Agree to disagree*
Disagreements will always happen in relationships. He should avoid fighting; it only fuels the fire and we always end up saying something that we really don't mean. Hurtful things happen when we fight; he should stay as far away from that as possible. Not every couple is going to agree on everything. Successful couples agree to disagree. If it is not a life-threatening matter, he should just let it go.

- *Compromise*
Ah, where would this world be without compromise? Nowhere. That is exactly where his relationship will end up if he doesn't practice compromise.

- *Communication*
This is a vital success factor in any relationship. How is he supposed to know what his partner is thinking or what is going on in their lives if there is no communication? Did you know that most arguments or disagreements between couples generally stem from a lack of communication? The best way to improve communication with his partner is to involve them in his world—especially his professional world.

- *Listening*
He should give his partner full attention and really listen. There is nothing more annoying than talking to someone's back. Hearing is not the same as listening. He should always try to understand issues from his partner's perspective; he shouldn't overreact or become defensive. Relationships need such listening.

To reiterate a very important message, after he has established a strong relationship, he should proactively manage it. Just because things are okay right now doesn't mean they will remain that way. Things can change suddenly and could cost him dearly. The most important area for him to focus on is communication.

Over-Communicate

Lack of communication is a huge issue in relationships, especially in this era of trying to do more with less. Who has the time to have meaningful and constructive conversations? Your son does. He has no choice—he should just do it!

Below are several tips on how your son should communicate with his partner:

- *Schedule a date night once a week*
  Whether it's thirty minutes or five hours, find time at night to talk—with the TV off.

- *Never go to sleep during a heated argument*
  Make every possible effort to resolve it. Don't let it drag on for days or weeks.

- *Learn to give in*
  He should learn to say I am sorry—even if it's not his fault. It doesn't matter who's to blame. He has too many other things to worry about.

- *Try to listen to your partner*
  Don't interrupt, even if it's a heated discussion and even if the discussion is baseless and doesn't make any sense. Let them get it all out and pay attention to what they're saying instead of how they're saying it.

- *Don't bring up past negative incidents*
  Things that happened in the past are irrelevant. They will only make the current situation worse.

- *Choose your words carefully*
  You never know when a certain word could be taken the wrong way—don't take a chance of being misunderstood. Sometimes a normal discussion of

a sensitive issue can get ugly quickly. Just like you choose your words carefully in the corporate world, there is no difference here—be politically astute!

- *Be respectful at all times*
  Don't mock or belittle. Listen conscientiously and value your partner's opinion. Be kind, soft-spoken, and well-mannered.

- *Find a quiet place to have discussions*
  No TV or loud noise.

- *Before discussing a sensitive issue—don't just blurt out the problem—provide a solution first*
  For example, he shouldn't just tell his partner that she never cooks dinner. Suggest, instead, that they schedule a time to cook together.

- *Winning an argument is irrelevant*
  Don't go there.

- *Respect your partner at all times*
  Treat your partner as you wish to be treated. No name-calling, no sarcasm, no teasing—always highlight their strengths.

- *Always be honest*
  Lies beget lies.

- *Don't cause a disturbance*
  Yelling, throwing something, hitting something, or storming out of a room and slamming a door will only exacerbate a negative situation. Don't make a scene. Exercise to release tension and become calm.

- *It takes two to tango*
  Look for common ground during arguments—learn to give in. Look for positive scenarios.

He should be proactive with his partner for personal and professional issues. After living with someone for a long time, most of us take good communication practices for granted—especially for what we may consider to be an insignificant issue. It might be a sore spot for his partner. Whether it's keeping his personal life in harmony by proactively communicating or networking with key executives to improve his stature in the workplace, communication is the key ingredient for success for any relationship.

He needs to bring 'her' into his world

If your son is an over-achiever and becoming highly successful, it's going to be difficult to keep his partner abreast of his work activities, especially on a regular basis. He should make every attempt to summarize what's happening to his partner.

If he's managing the finances for the household, he should always update his partner. He should share a formal document on a spreadsheet, which they can both review together. They should review the status of their finances at least monthly. While reviewing their finances together, they should discuss goals, priorities, and vacations. It's important to develop a strong union.

Chapter 6

Self-Discipline

A scholastic genius, but could fail the test of life

Great, Alex aced History, Math, Government, and many other challenging courses. Heck, she even aced French and Spanish. I was very proud of her, but at the same time I knew that mastering her high school curriculum was secondary to understanding how to manage her life as an adult; but I couldn't mention that because I wanted her to only focus on her GPA.

Throughout her tenure in junior high school and high school, I mouthed off the words, *"It's all about your GPA,"* but that's where I stopped pontificating. Subconsciously, I knew that it would be a huge effort to help her be disciplined and look at life as an adult versus one big virtual playground. I also knew that she didn't have to put forth much energy into acing her high school courses because they were fairly easy. Academically she was bright. Nonacademic intelligence didn't exist. What good is it for Alex to graduate high school with a 4.0 GPA when she couldn't manage herself? I would gladly trade in some of those academic smarts of hers for some common sense and to acquire some level of discipline.

What does that mean?
- Being focused on goals and waking up with a purpose every day
- Being structured (organized, following a to-do list, consistently following a routine) for efficiency
- Maintaining a healthy lifestyle by eating right and exercising daily
- Living life with urgency
- Holding yourself accountable
- Managing finances effectively
- Adhering to the most critical priorities
- Managing time effectively
  - Not procrastinating

Life is challenging—no, it's a bitch, to put it bluntly, but most of you already know that. That message needs to be articulated to your son repeatedly until it sinks in. If he can't manage his life effectively, it's almost impossible to succeed—he'll be lucky to survive each day. Is that what you want for your son? To exist or to live? He will struggle for the rest of his life.

So I ask again, what good is your son's schooling if he can't:

- Motivate himself consistently
- Manage his sleep optimally
- Maneuver (in the politically correct manner) in the corporate world
- Strategize to improve efficiency
- Manage his finances
- Interview for a job in the appropriate manner
- Manage his health
- Set and manage personal and professional goals
- Perform consistently at a high level
- Prioritize

What do you think is going to happen when he enters his thirties and forties and he's not disciplined? The problems will only intensify. You know these issues don't go away with maturity. Children are taught at a very young age how to be structured in school. They have a set schedule, and they must comply or get reprimanded. So why can't most teens propagate that structure into other areas of their life, especially after school? You don't have to look or think too hard, the #1 reason is because they're undisciplined and are incapable of holding themselves accountable.

In most instances siblings mimic you, but unfortunately, you're not setting the proper example by turning off your devices after getting home. Instead of spending quality time with your family, you're preoccupied with work. It's easy for you to play Monday-morning quarterback and criticize your son when you're doing the same thing. It's difficult because employers are pushing harder on their employees to constantly do more with less. But I had no choice, and neither do you. We must help our teens develop critical adult skills.

You know the importance of being disciplined; do you want your bad traits to be passed on to your son? Based on hundreds of life coaching real life scenarios, you waste approximately four hours a day. It's much easier to be unstructured and lazy than it is to be structured and live efficiently and accomplish as much as possible. Don't let your lethargic lifestyle rub off on your son.

Being disciplined is the defining element in your life.
With it you can achieve almost anything; without it,
you witl struggle to exist.
—Harris Kern

Helping your son develop his self-discipline is a key component for success. It allowed me to establish my legacy and financial security for my family. If he is disciplined, he will be efficient, have endless drive, stay focused on his priorities, be strong (mentally and physically), and have an endless appetite to accomplish more. I wanted Alex to acquire this gift. She needed it in the worst way, as highlighted by many of her weaknesses noted earlier.

Being disciplined is many things, but above all, it is about establishing self–confidence. This level of self-assurance does not happen overnight. Once your son becomes disciplined, that conviction cannot be shattered regardless of any obstacle or turmoil in his life. It is a tool to help him accomplish whatever he desires!

It is also so much more. Being disciplined brings with it a completely new outlook on life. Even if your son has a bad day or week, being disciplined will keep him thinking positively. The worse things get, his discipline will motivate him to focus on his daily obligations. It harnesses the negative attitude into a positive force that helps him produce solutions to resolve the issues.

Once he establishes goals and sets milestones, the daily challenge begins. Being disciplined is a contract with himself. A contract he must follow, regardless of the circumstances. It becomes the cop on his shoulder: break the rule, and you fail. I forwarded the quote below to Alex and told her to think about looking hard at the reflection of herself in the mirror.

The Man in the Glass

When you get what you want in your struggle for self
And the world makes you king for a day
Just go to the mirror and look at yourself
And see what that man has to say.

For it isn't your father, or mother, or wife
Whose judgment upon you must pass
The fellow whose verdict counts most in your life
Is the one staring back from the glass.

He's the fellow to please—never mind all the rest
For he's with you, clear to the end
And you've passed your most difficult, dangerous test
If the man in the glass is your friend.

You may fool the whole world down the pathway of years
And get pats on the back as you pass
But your final reward will be heartache and tears
If you've cheated the man in the glass.

Peter Dale Wimbrow Sr.

The message is quite simple. Having discipline equates to being productive when she looks at that reflection. The message behind the image in the mirror is the foundation for acquiring discipline. She must continuously challenge herself. This is a full–time commitment, 7 days a week, 365 days a year. It cannot be accomplished with a part–time effort. That is why so many people fail in their attempts to be disciplined. It must be part of her daily routine, just like putting clothes on in the morning or eating a meal. Acquiring discipline will mean dramatically changing her lifestyle. Whether she is 20, 30, or 60 years old, with discipline she can be successful in everything she does.

Another important message from the mirror is that she should open the door to her mind everyday and take a snapshot of the goals she wants to accomplish. The thing to remember when going down this path is not to just merely achieve her goals on schedule—never just "meet" a goal's completion date. The objective is to shatter that goal. She should always try to outperform her previous best. Her competition is only that reflection. She has to judge her progress by no one else's standards or accomplishments. That's what it takes to acquire discipline: a constant one-on-one dialogue. Being disciplined will be a constant battle with herself, and the reflection is her enemy—her greatest challenge. I tell Alex all the time, *"Look in the mirror and always tell yourself: it's me, myself and I."* It is also very important for her to consistently remind herself that the body and mind must be one powerful force. She cannot separate the two. To separate the two will surely mean failure. Her body needs her mind, and her mind needs her body. She needs to take care of both. Yes, that means exercising and eating right. She needs the whole package behind her to be successful. Below was a discussion Alex and I had to develop her self-discipline skills. One day she came to me and said: *"Daddy, I think I have ADD. My girlfriend and I did some research, and the symptoms for ADD sound exactly like the same symptoms I have. It's the main reason I can't focus and get distracted easily."* Below was my response, which I emailed, printed, and made sure she read it in front of me.

Real Life Scenario: Self-Discipline vs. ADD/ADHD

"Alex, I'm not pretending to be a medical expert, I'm just your father who loves you dearly and is trying to keep you focused on your education. I'm basing my comments (below) on research I've compiled about ADD and ADHD, working with my life coaching clients over the years, being a self-discipline master, and witnessing your mode of operation every day. As always, my opinion is unbiased and based solely on facts.

One of the most overly used phrases during the past decade is: I think I have ADD or ADHD. It's easier to blame your personal and professional deficiencies on some medical prognoses rather than recognizing the root cause of the problem, which is a major addiction to your smartphone. You can't stop looking at it day or night. You actually fall asleep with it in your hand every night. You study with your cell on, and you're constantly replying to text messages from one of your four close friends. You also get text messages from other acquaintances throughout the week. When you're not replying to countless text messages, you're thinking about your ex-boyfriend, weekend activities, playing on Snapchat or futzing with music on your cellular. There are probably a half-dozen other distractions as well. If we switched roles and I was Alex and you were watching my behavior with these antics, you would shake your head in disbelief. Now hear this loud and clear: you can NOT focus until you turn ALL distractions off.

A few weeks back, we had a serious discussion on your lack of focus and the fact that you are easily distracted with subjects that are more challenging and require extra study time, i.e., college AP courses you've been taking in your senior year of high school. The situation is critical because you flunked one college course, and you're on the verge of doing the same with Economics AP.

Do you know what most experts say? You need to be more structured (organized); improve your time management by setting deadlines for everything, even the smallest tasks. You also need to get on a regular sleep schedule and make exercise part of your daily routine. The only area you comply with is perhaps your sleep schedule, but you still try and study the hard stuff at night before you go to sleep. You cannot study brain intense material when your brain is tired.

With the help of a structured lifestyle, which you do NOT have, you can instill change. You don't necessarily need outside professional intervention—at least not right away. There is a lot you can do to help get your symptoms under control. The choice is yours, but this is the last time I will waste precious resources if you do not listen.

If you want to change your life for the better and have a chance of being a successful adult, then follow my recommendations:

- Turn off your cellular phone while studying, but also leave it in a different room—you are too addicted— even seeing it is a distraction. Trust me, your friends are NOT the priority. Alex's studies are the priority!
- If possible, do all brain intense activities in the morning when you're well rested, especially your studies.
- Follow your morning and evening routine.
- Adhere to your to-do list.
- Be organized at all times.
- Stop procrastinating and wasting time.
- Stop listening to your friends regarding personal and professional development. They simply do not have a clue.

Here's my proposition: implement all of these recommendations immediately and maintain them for 90 days. If they work, great; if not, then I will take you to the doctor, but remember their so-called cures only have a 50% success rate and taking those meds have some strong side effects.

You're running out of time; your senior year is already 6 weeks old, and as it stands right now, you're not ready for college. Your dream has always been to attend college. PLEASE don't let this addiction destroy your future."

After Alex read this note, she remained quiet. She really didn't know what to say. It was a look I've never seen before. I decided to remain quiet until the next morning when I approached her and said, "Good morning, love."

"Good morning, Daddy."

"You haven't said a word about my note."

"I know, it's because I am angry at myself for being so lazy and not being able to focus."

"Would you like me to tell you where to begin to fix your laziness?"

"Yes."

"Okay, let's simplify the process of instilling some discipline into your life so you can motivate yourself and be more efficient. How does that sound?"

"It sounds good, thank you, Daddy."

Below is the process I taught Alex on how to acquire some much needed self-discipline.

Build and Execute

In order to sell my methodology to Alex and other teens, I had to dramatically simplify the steps required to develop self-discipline. I needed an anecdote that was easy to digest—just enough to hit the mark and quickly.

Below is the two-step process I used on Alex and a few other teens who lacked self-discipline:

1. *Build (the foundation)*
    a. Institute structure: Follow a morning and evening routine, be organized, and adhere to a to-do list
    b. Set priorities, goals, and milestones

2. *Execute*
    a. The most effective way to operate at a high level and hold yourself accountable consistently is to train your mind

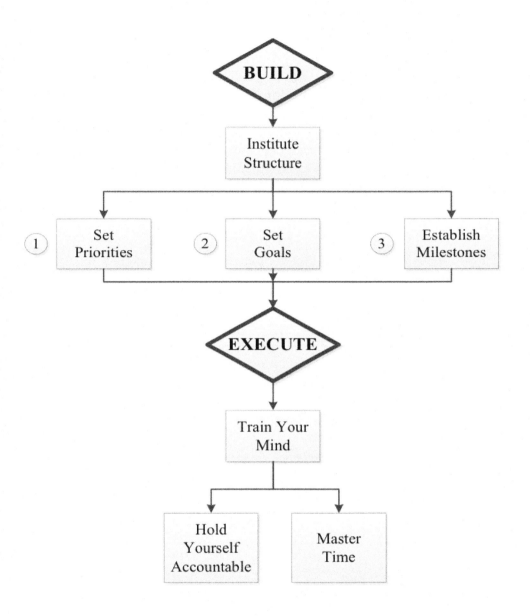

There are actually five steps, which are highlighted in the book titled *Going From Undisciplined to Self-Mastery: Five Simple Steps To Get You There*, but I felt that I needed to simplify it further for teens.

Build (The Foundation)

A well-built home has a solid foundation. For personal development that foundation is structure. To develop self-discipline, you need to institute structure first. Once your son gets organized, adheres to a routine, and follows a to-do list, then he can set priorities, goals, and milestones, knowing that his resources will be focused on what truly matters. Below is a graph depicting the build process.

Efficiency Starts With Structure

Help your son get structured. If he's not structured, his life will be chaotic and inefficient, therefore, unproductive. There's no way he could be efficient, living and working in cluttered environments. That includes his mind: when it's cluttered with too many things, he won't be able to focus on his goals.

Remain Organized

Alex did her studies in one of three areas: our home library, on the floor in my office (don't ask me why. . .), or on her bed. She used to leave her stuff around everywhere, which is typical for most teens, but over time she realized the benefits of keeping her work area neat and organized.

Eventually she used that same mentality (structure for efficiency) for other areas in her life like e-mail. The more clutter she had in her view and in her mind, the less productive she was. The more organized she was, the less time she wasted. The less time she wasted, the more productive she became—it was that simple.

Establish a To-Do List Nightly

"He who every morning plans the transactions of that day and follows that plan carries a thread that will guide him through the labyrinth of the most busy life."
Victor Hugo

Have your son document a list of activities (i.e., tasks, errands, spiritual activities, personal obligations, projects, etc.) the night before. He should establish one to-do list daily, which encompasses his professional and personal life. Below are some helpful tips you can teach him when establishing a to-do list.

Do not waste cycles in the morning
Teach your son to hit the ground running and make things happen immediately—when he wakes up. Most people waste precious cycles trying to remember what they need to do when they first get out of bed. It's much easier and more efficient to glance over at your to-do list and make things happen immediately and throughout the day.

As you know, teenagers are notorious for lounging around in bed until the last possible moment. As a parent, this is where you have to put your foot down. Stop babying your son, and force this issue to make sure he gets out of bed in a timely manner.

There are no negotiations here. Establish a routine that includes the time he needs to be out of bed.

Establish a Daily Routine

I helped Alex document an effortless routine. It's always best to keep things simple.

During the school week she would:
- Get up at 7:15 a.m. and review to-do list.
- Wash face, brush teeth, and make the bed.
- Be downstairs by 7:30 a.m. Have breakfast and do daily household chores (cleaning the table, putting the dishes away, and tidying up the living room and kitchen areas).
- Be back upstairs at 8 a.m. and prep for school (makeup, brush hair, tidy up bath room, and bring down dirty laundry).
- Be in the car by 8:30 a.m. for school.

At the very least, your son should follow a morning and evening routine for the week and one for the weekend. He needs to keep his routine simple. The more complex it is, the more difficult it will be to follow consistently. Below is a discussion I had with Alex on the benefits of being structured.

Real Life Scenario: Living a Structured Lifestyle

She was like most teens—disorganized. She was efficient at school, but not as much after school; she wasted precious resources and rarely completed her daily responsibilities. My mission was to show her the advantages of living a structured lifestyle and that it would make her twice as efficient, but that alone wasn't enough of an incentive to convince her to forego her fly-by-the-seat-of-her-pants lifestyle.

Then I said something that caught her attention:

"If you're more efficient, it means you can complete your responsibilities faster and then spend more time with your friends."

Now that captured her interest.

"Do you want me to show you how?"
"Okay"
"Tell me your obligations for today."

While she was rambling off her list, I wrote them down on my 8.5 x11 legal notepad:

- Work on my English project that's due in two days.
- Read my Economics AP chapter in preparation for a quiz.
- Begin working on my English essay.
- Bring my dirty laundry downstairs.
- Clean our home gym.
- Clean the kitchen table.
- Reply to Sophie's long text message.
- Go to the gym with Daddy.
- Fix my bed and tidy up the bathroom.

"Here you go. Follow this throughout the day and cross off each item with this black marker when you've completed each item."

She took it and said, "Thank you."

A key success factor was included: activities with her friends, which was important to her; otherwise, the to-do list would have gone nowhere. It still wasn't enough to guarantee she would remain structured. We monitored progress to ensure she was holding herself accountable. A similar routine was established for the weekend. It was more flexible, as I let her stay up late Friday and Saturday nights to speak with her friends and watch movies. She slept in on Saturday and Sunday morning, but when she woke up, she adhered to her routine and to-do list. I made structure a major part of her life, and eventually, she did it automatically without having checkpoints.

Set Priorities, Goals and Milestones

Life is hectic, demanding, and stressful at times. If your son thinks he has it rough now, he hasn't seen anything yet. Trying to manage his future family, spiritual obligations, career responsibilities, exercise regimen, and friends without prioritizing is futile. The odds of success are greatly improved if he tackles his daily obligations in a well-planned and structured manner. Once his life is structured, then he can establish priorities, goals, and milestones.

The most critical priorities to focus on are:

- *Finances*: Managing finances (income, expenses, savings, and investments)
- *Career*: Job, business, and education
- *Health*: Exercise, weight management, lifestyle (drinking, smoking, etc.)
- *Relationships*: Spiritual with God, managing emotions and your significant other, spending quality time with family, allocating time for friends, and managing professional relationships

Focusing on these priorities consistently will have your son living a rewarding, happy, and fulfilled life. Once priorities have been set, then he can establish goals with milestones.

The hierarchy would look like:

1. Priority#1
    a. Goal#1
    b. Milestone#1
        i. Milestone#2
        ii. Milestone#3
    b. Goal#2
        i. Milestone#1
        ii. Milestone#2

2. Priority#2
    a. Goal#1
        i. Milestone#1

The graphic below depicts a different view of the hierarchy for effective goal management.

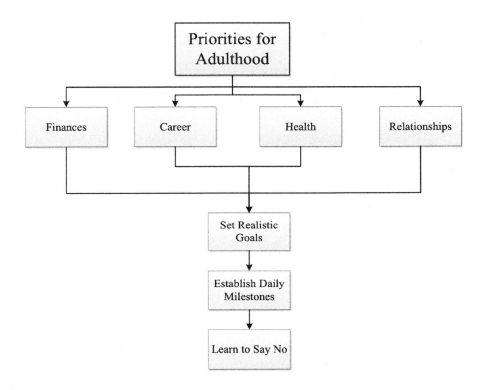

Focus on the Rocks Instead of the Pebbles

It's easy to get into a rut. To get buried in the day-to-day activities that are essential, but do very little to help *you* accomplish your *major* goals and grow. These actions I refer to as chasing *pebbles*. Most of us have a long list of pebbles to do every day, especially us parents. If you're constantly enmeshed in activities that are important to the family's well-being, but do very little to help you grow as an individual, then you will most likely be unfulfilled. Don't let this happen to your son.

Establish *rock* time in his daily routine. Help him strategize on the big stuff that's all about his development before the pebble chasing begins. The *pebble-chasing* will never stop and will only grow as his family does. Unfortunately, it's the only way to focus on his *major* goals. For me, the rocks are my prayers, business, writing, and exercise routine. These must be accomplished daily to feel productive and satisfied. Everyone has different rocks;

focus on them. It's easy to get into a groove; those errands, obligations, friend drama, etc., and lose sight of the bigger things. Once he finds those rocks, ensure that he focuses on them via his daily routine and to-do list. If he completes his rock activities for the day, the pebbles won't be as laborious. Below is one of my favorite quotes:

A philosophy professor stood before his class and had some items in front of him. When class began, wordlessly he picked up a large empty mayonnaise jar and proceeded to fill it with rocks right to the top, rocks about 2" diameter. He then asked the students if the jar was full?

They agreed that it was. So the professor then picked up a box of pebbles and poured them in to the jar. He shook the jar lightly. The pebbles, of course, rolled into the open areas between the rocks. The students laughed. He asked his students again if the jar was full?

They agreed that yes, it was. The professor then picked up a box of sand and poured it into the jar. Of course, the sand filled up everything else.

"Now," said the professor, "I want you to recognize that this is your life. The rocks are the important things - your family, your partner, your health, your children - anything that is so important to you that if it were lost, you would be nearly destroyed.

The pebbles are the other things in life that matter, but on a smaller scale. The pebbles represent things like your job, your house, your car.

The sand is everything else. The small stuff. If you put the sand or the pebbles into the jar first, there is no room for the rocks. The same goes for your life.

If you spend all your energy and time on the small stuff, material things, you will never have room for the things that are truly most important.

Pay attention to the things that are critical in your life. Play with your children. Take your partner out dancing There will always be time to go to work, clean the house, give a dinner party, and fix the disposal.

Take care of the rocks first—the things that really matter."

Set Realistic and Conservative Goals Initially

Very few people ever achieve their goals and reap the benefits—the rewards are second to none. Earlier in the book I discussed how I helped Alex set realistic and conservative goals. Formal goal management is a foreign concept to all teens, but also for most adults. I spent quite a bit of time making sure Alex's goals were aligned with her priorities, and milestones were established for each goal with realistic due dates. She needed to feel successes, and if she took on too much, she would have failed. Once your son starts developing self-discipline and holding himself accountable, he can gradually take on more.

Dreams, goals, ambitions—these are the stuff man uses for fuel.

—L. Ron Hubbard
U.S. author & science fiction novelist (1911 - 1986)

In the absence of clearly defined goals, we become strangely loyal to performing daily trivia until ultimately we become enslaved by it.

—Robert Heinlein
U.S. science fiction author (1907 - 1988)

These two quotes say it all. If you don't have goals, you wind up having no life. If you do have goals to shoot for, then you have the fuel and the drive to achieve and find happiness. So proper goal management is key to long-term satisfaction.

One day Alex informed me (actually blindsided me) that she wanted to buy a car, and she also wanted to move out with her friends as soon as possible—that was all—wow, my poor head was spinning. Typical 18-year-old teenage nonsense. Why was it nonsense? Because I knew that my lovely daughter and her friends didn't plan everything thoroughly, especially the financial aspect of this equation.

These are all sensitive issues and needed to be discussed in person, but I also wanted to write everything down so I wouldn't forget to mention something important or be blindsided and let her highly volatile emotions derail our discussions. Below is my reply back to her newest wants. I emailed her the following note after I printed it out and discussed it in person.

Real Life Scenario: Setting Pie-in-the-sky Goals

Dear Alex,

This is your dear old dad, who loves you immensely and wants to see you happy and successful as an adult, more than anyone else (especially before I leave this planet). Do you know why? Because I know what success feels like, very few will ever proclaim that sensation, which is why I am writing to your desires to move out and buy a car. My only request is that you read this slowly, carefully, and objectively.

I began writing this note after you recently texted me to help you buy a car—you were researching used cars on autotrader.com—do you remember that day? I texted you back and mentioned that I was busy working on a critical project at the moment, and I would discuss it with you in a few days. You've also been talking about moving out with your friends in the next few months. My response encapsulates the issues with your latest desires and provides you with possible solutions.

Your latest goals +

Besides these two new major goals, I decided to expand our discussion to include an important issue: you stopped exercising, and still, always put your genuinely caring heart before your pocketbook for your friends, which is admirable, but not wise if you want to accomplish these two goals. Also, I'm not going to say no to anything you want; that's not my role. My job is to present the facts and let you make a decision. I will forego most of the car conversation for now, as it warrants a separate discussion.

The Issues

Buying a good used car (the key word is good) and moving out at the same time require additional funds. Unfortunately, the math doesn't add up—you don't earn enough. You would need to make at least $1500.00—$2000.00 more a month. Just recently you purchased tickets ($173.00) to attend a concert with your friends, which is fine because it was your first one, you also bought a tote bag and wrist band at the concert ($20.00), got a tattoo for yourself ($60.00), bought your friend lunch, then you mentioned that: "Sophie's birthday is next month, and I need to buy her something." In other words, the spending on the small stuff will continue. Unfortunately, if you keep spending on the small stuff, it will take you much longer to attain your major goals.

The second, even bigger problem is that you're constantly getting distracted, and you're a severe procrastinator, which is something we both recognize and you've stated in the past. Do you honestly think that you can live in a house with several friends and focus on your studies? We all know the answer to this question is a resounding no.

Possible Solutions

You know I've always tried to broker a deal with you and never just say no; however, now it's time for Daddy to interject a major dose of reality. In life we can't always have everything we want, especially at once without prioritizing and without sacrifice, but there is hope, and you can eventually make it all happen if you plan and execute in a structured and conservative manner (taking small steps forward). Stay the course; don't try to take on the world and do everything at once and probably fail. One of the main reasons people don't accomplish their goals is because they try and do too much at the same time and fail at all of them.

I mentioned earlier that you stopped exercising, which was a huge mistake. Do you remember how happy you were when you squatted your weight? Exercise is paramount to maintain good health and give you the energy and stamina to excel in life. Another added benefit is that it gives you a positive outlook every time you finish one of your exercise routines, and it consistently builds confidence. This will help you deal with your low self-esteem; besides, your cute little 18-year-old body won't be so cute as you age, but if you exercise consistently, it will look good much longer.

Here's what I recommend, but you don't have to agree:

1. *Get that high GPA in your senior year of high school. This should be top priority, but you need to turn your cellular off while studying. Once again, I said it earlier, but it deserves repeating, you are easily distracted. Trust me, sweetheart—turn off all distractions until you finish your priorities on any given day.*

2. *Reduce your expenditures and save every penny. This includes spending money on gifts for your friends on momentous occasions, like birthdays. Take them to a matinee that will cost you half the price of those evening showings, then hang out together at home and watch Netflix in our theatre, which I'm sure they would love to do, or you can go to Subway and have an inexpensive lunch. They will certainly understand that you desperately want to save money for a car.*

3. *Forego the thought of buying a car until you graduate high school. As long as I am driving you to work each day, take advantage of me and continue saving your money. Besides, you know it will be a huge distraction. Upon graduating high school and obtaining that elite score, I will loan you some money to purchase a good car. If you remain frugal, you can probably double your funds in your savings account. You currently have $4K in savings; if you reach $7K or $8K by the end of your senior year, we will shop for a car. I will loan you the remaining $2-3K so you can buy a good one, but the loan comes with a few stipulations: It must be paid back in full, and it's the first payment you make each month.*

4. *Stop thinking about moving out until you graduate from college. Continue to save money. Moving out in a few years is not the end of the world. You have*

a good life, young lady, and you live in a beautiful home in a upper middle class neighborhood. When you eventually purchase that car, you can visit your friends more frequently. Consider moving out after you graduate from community college.

5. *Exercise at least two days a week consistently. This is a very conservative and realistic goal, mainly due to your work and school schedule. Go to the gym one day a week with me, and since you enjoy walking, do that once a week. This will not only keep you healthier and energetic, but also build confidence.*

6. *Focus more on Alex and less on your friends. Unfortunately, your mentality at this stage of your development should be: me, myself and I (except for God and family), because in the end, your friends will have their own families with their issues to deal with and, probably, will live in a different city or state. They will still be your friends, but they won't have time to text you for hours, as they do now.*

If you agree to items 1-6 above, I will continue to mentor you. If not, I will stop, and you can do as you wish. Just remember that my love for you is eternal—this will never change. The choice is yours.

On a final note, just about everything I mention above requires money, so please don't be like the fools that say money is not that important. I beg to differ; this world revolves around money, which is sad to report.

Love You,
Daddy
After I had her read this in front of me, I asked her, "What do you think?"

She wasn't smiling so I was bracing myself for the worst, but after a few seconds she said, "You're right, Daddy."

"I'd like to share a very important reason why so many people don't accomplish their goals."

"What is that?"

"People love to babble, like you."

"But, I don't want to be rude, daddy."

"You don't have to be impolite, sweetheart, but you need to learn how to turn the babble around you off or you will have a difficult time completing your goals. Next to poor self-discipline, which is the number one time waster because people do a poor job of managing themselves, the number two goal stopper is listening to insignificant babble. I will teach you how to tune it out without saying the no word."

"Thank you, daddy."

Below is the discussion I had with Alex the next day on how to politely cutoff irrelevant babble.

Real Life Scenario: Learning to Say No

"Alex, as we were discussing yesterday, people can gobble up many of your available resources in a hurry. Time is valuable, and everyone I know of has more to do than time available. If you try to help everyone and take on too much, you will surely fail. Does this make sense?"

"Yes, it does, Daddy."

"As with small expenditures, don't look at it as if it was a one-time occurrence or with time like it was only a few minutes; extrapolate every 5- or 10-minute conversation throughout the year and see how much time you actually waste. It will shock your system."

"Wouldn't you rather invest that time into your goals or chatting with your close friends?"

"Yes, I would."

"People will utilize a huge chunk of your resources, i.e., listening to irrelevant conversations, drama-plagued individuals, or people that are too detail-oriented.

"You will need to cut detail-oriented people off politely in their conversations. Help those babblers get to the point faster. Don't be rude, but you can certainly cut them off in a respectful manner.

Below are a few tips on how to cut people off politely while at work:

- *Tell little white lies*

Make excuses (i.e., I have a crucial meeting to attend that my boss just unexpectedly announced).

- *Don't have lengthy conversations with colleagues*
  In the hallway, break room, etc., unless it benefits her career—then by all means she should schmooze with them."

"Okay, Daddy I will try it."

She stopped asking to buy a car and move out, managed her finances scrupulously and reduced babbling time considerably.

Execute (Consistently)

Consistently completing your goals can only be achieved by training your mind. Most people do not train their mind, therefore are inconsistent. Once your mind is trained and you are holding yourself accountable, you will be operating at an efficient level—never procrastinating again. Read below for details on how to train your mind to hold yourself accountable.

How to Hold Yourself Accountable: What is Accountability

Holding yourself accountable is where the rubber meets the road. It's where most people fail in their self-development efforts. Therefore, I've divided accountability into three parts because it's important to first teach your son *what* accountability is, then how to attain it, and finally, what the end result looks like. Below is a depiction of what accountability is.

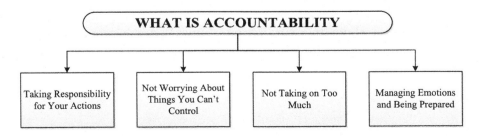

Just like most adults, Alex arbitrarily said yes, but she rarely followed through with her commitments. Below is a conversation I had with her one day because she dropped the ball on something, yet again.

Real Life Scenario: Taking Responsibility for Your Actions

"Alex, you need to stop saying yes and not delivering—it's annoying. I've asked you four times in the past few days to iron my shirts, and each time you negated. I am tired of asking. You need to take responsibility for your actions."

"I'm sorry, I'll do it, Daddy."

"Yeah, right, those three words carry very little substance; sure, your intentions are good, but that won't help you in life. Commitment cannot be halfhearted, for that is not commitment. It needs to be all out. Your mind and body have to want it and be completely behind it. Once you commit to something, you need to follow through. Where would society be without accountability? Our society is highly efficient and depends on people to be accountable for their actions from businesses, transportation systems, and schools. Without accountability there would be chaos. We have to eat and pay our bills; we have no choice. Unfortunately, accountability stops there for many, including you. The only way to truly hold yourself accountable 24/7 is to train your mind until it ensures you comply."

"How do you train your mind?"

"I will teach you shortly, but first, there are a few other things you need to know."

Before I could help Alex train her mind, she had to do a better job of managing time. She felt obligated to help her friends with their issues and drama instead of worrying about her priorities and dealing with her emotions. Below is one of many conversations Alex and I had regarding poor time management.

Real Life Scenario: Wasting Time Dealing With Irrelevance

"Alex, time is limited, and you worry about too many insignificant things."

"What do you mean?"

"Don't worry about things you can't control. Whether it's related to school, work, or your ex-boyfriend who already has a different agenda, you're wasting precious cycles. Why bother when sometimes there's nothing you can do about the situation. Whether it was one of your teachers who didn't teach in the manner you preferred or your boss who was a micro-manager. There was nothing you could do about any of these issues; however, it would always upset you, and then countless hours were wasted worrying about those situations."

"I know, but it's not that easy to stop thinking about these things sometimes."

"I will teach you how, but first you have to stop embracing the nonsense. The things that are out of your control and spending an exorbitant amount of time listening to your friend's problems."

"I will try, Daddy."

"Alex, be prudent about how much you undertake. Stop being so accommodating; you already have a full plate. If you have ample time at the end of the day and you're not that tired, then perhaps you can take on more."

"But my friends are always texting or calling me when they have problems with their boyfriends."

"If you keep helping them with their issues, then you will never complete your goals and for what—their drama? Wise up, Alex; babbling about someone else's nonsense will get you nowhere in life. If it was an emergency, that's different, but for small talk or drama about their latest boyfriend problem—don't go there. Ask yourself: when do most of your friends call you? Let me answer that: it's when they have problems with their boyfriends—right?"

"But I feel bad for them; they're really down and need to speak with someone."

"They'll get over it, and you'll be able to focus on Alex and her goals. Listen, your girlfriends will have many boyfriends and probably will go through several husbands later in life. It's sad to say, but more than half the marriages end up in divorce—those are real statistics."

"What?"

"Yes, so please stop wasting so much time listening to their endless drama. Next time, which will probably be in the next day or so, if one of them calls and wants to talk to you about issues with their boyfriend, tell them that you have tons of homework and you will try to call them back, but don't, and focus on Alex's priorities."

"But I feel obliged to call them back because I said I would."

"Yes, of course, but text them back instead and apologize that you can't speak with them because of your homework and home chores. You can also use me as the primary reason you can't talk. Remember, always take care of Alex and her obligations first, and never over-commit."

"Okay, Daddy."

It wasn't that easy, and it took a long time, but eventually she realized that I was right, and that her friends and their drama was last on life's pecking order.

Managing Negative Emotions

Half the time life is good, and half the time it's downright ugly. This is reality. Your son won't always be able to predict when bad times rear their ugly head—there's no way to control many negative situations. Teach him how to prepare for the worst of times. Those bad days *will* blindside him regardless of how positive he may feel on any given day. For most teens parents shelter them from some of the more challenging and downright ugly situations. Eventually your son will need to endure all negative scenarios by himself. The responsibilities are enormous; the pressure to survive and excel as an adult are stressful at times. He will need to learn how to train his mind to deal with negative situations. Controlling and redirecting negative emotions into positive energy is paramount for his future.

Alex and her highly emotional episodes and constant drama were strenuous, to say the least. She was worrying about her education, career, boys, friends, just to mention a few. During one of those rare weeks out of the month when she wasn't so emotional, I decided to approach her to discuss how I could provide insight to help manage her emotions. Below is our conversation.

Real Life Scenario: Managing Negative Emotions

"Alex, you're really happy today."

"Yes, Daddy, it's a wonderful day. I had a great evening at work last night."

"I wish you were this happy all the time, but that's not always possible, is it?"

"No, it's not."

"I would love to see more emotion-neutral days." I said it as if I was kidding, but I wasn't, and she picked up on it, too.

"I know, it's not easy living with a teenage girl, Daddy."

"Yup, but I wouldn't have it any other way. You just need to manage your emotions. It's important that you learn to maintain an even-keel demeanor every day (not getting too excited or too upset). This will help you prepare for the unexpected, especially for the worst of times. Good and bad things will always happen, regardless of your disposition and how hopeful you are on any given day. If something negative brings you down, the best thing you can do is to redirect your energy toward your priorities, instead of dwelling on the negativity."

"What do you mean by that, Daddy?" she said as she looked at me with a blank stare.

"Bad days are part of life, and many times the issues will be out of your control; they will bring you down and stop you in your tracks. You won't feel like doing anything; you will just be an emotional wreck. There are several methods you can use to move forward and be productive. Focus on your priorities and to-do list and leverage God. Whenever you feel down, turn to Him immediately and thank Him for the way you feel over and over again until you feel better. On good days thank Him for your happiness."

"Managing your emotions means being prepared and planning for worst-case scenarios. Emergencies happen when you least expect them. Negativity comes unexpectedly, regardless of what you say or do to remain positive. The more practice you get controlling your emotions, the easier it will be to cope with the unexpected. There's an old saying: Stay positive, and good things will happen. Nice concept, but it's not always true. Sure, you should think positive every day of the year, but that's not realistic over the long haul. Alex, do you ever see me get too excited or too depressed?"

"No."

"Do you know why?"

"Not really, I just figured you were way too manly."

I chuckled a bit and said, "I've trained my mind to always have an even-keel demeanor. It's a major success factor for me. If I let every little thing in my personal life get to me, do you honestly think I would have been so successful?"

"No, but how did you shut out those really bad days?"

"By pretending every day was a bad day and, eventually, I was prepared for anything good or bad. I became immune to everything except my priorities."

"But isn't that being really negative again?" she asked.

"I was only negative on the inside; no one suspected a thing, not even you—right?"

"Nope."

"There you have it. It's critical that you manage your emotions; otherwise, you will never accomplish your goals. Also, most down days are typically caused by a relationship breakup, and I will teach you how to deal with those situations below."

"Thanks, Daddy."

How Do You Hold Yourself Accountable: Training Your Mind

Teach your son to hold himself accountable consistently by training his mind to be his own cop. Once his mind is trained, it becomes that guiding force behind all of his actions; then and only then, he will realize the benefits. It will constantly nudge him forward even when he's tired, feeling lazy, or having a bad hair day.

There are three ways he can train his mind:

1. *Set an expiration date*
   He needs to play mind games until his mind is trained and he believes that he will die on set date. This will motivate him every day to live with a sense of urgency to always accomplish more. This method is difficult to teach teens because their motto is: what's the rush? However, to get the best and fastest results—this is my favorite method. My neighbor mentored me when I was 13 years old (over four decades ago) to live like I was going to die at the age of 40. The rewards were second to none; please refer to the About the Author section.

2. *Establish phrases (negative or positive affirmations)*
   Phrases that impact the way he thinks and operates. He needs to repeat those phrases throughout the day multiple times. For examples of positive and negative phrases, read the book titled *Live Like You Are Dying: Make Your Life Count Moment By Moment*. Repeating something enough eventually becomes habitual. This method is straightforward, but it does take effort and focus. Because his smartphone takes precedence over self-development, this method will also be difficult.

3. *Treat every day equally*
   This method is challenging but the odds of success are better. Having him adhere to a daily routine and a to-do list is achievable, and he will institute structure in his life. Once he gets structured, teach him how to live with urgency and to hold himself accountable.

I used all three methods (highlighted below) on Alex and my life coaching clients.

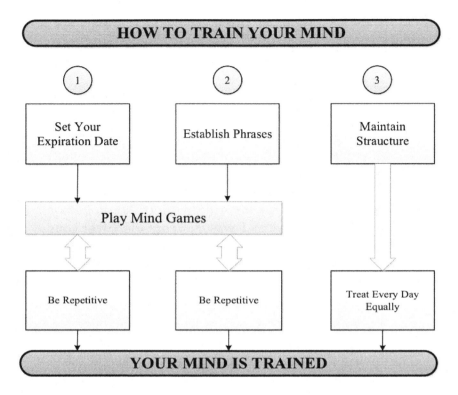

Set Your Expiration Date

One of the most effective methods for your son to be super productive is to have him train his mind by believing he has an expiration date, just like any carton of milk. Trust me, it works. I approached my mentor in my early twenties and asked him how I can *consistently* do more in a shorter amount of time. He said, "Train your mind to believe you are going to die soon." I looked at him like he had two heads instead of one, but never questioned him and never looked back.

Based on my major goals, I decided to pick the age of 40 as my last day on this planet. I kept telling myself repeatedly (actually several times a day) until I trained my mind and actually started to believe that I was going to die at 40. I wanted to give myself a deadline to complete my major goals as quickly as possible. I also wanted to leave behind a legacy for my future family. I've seen too many elderly people who had given up on their dreams, too many people with regrets because they didn't complete some of their most important goals. I didn't want to be another statistic. I pushed *hard*.

I actually accomplished the following major goals at the age of 38:

- Saved one million dollars in cash and owned one million dollars in assets.
- Owned three homes.
- Purchased a luxury car in cash.
- Promoted to a Vice President position in a major corporation.
- Traveled the world several times (logged over four million airline miles).
- Published a book.
- Built one of the top muscle cars in the nation. I was a muscle car and speedboat fanatic. I wanted to own the ultimate car and boat with matching paint jobs. They actually graced the cover of *Hot Rod Magazine* in July of 1975.

I'm not saying for your son to take it to this extreme; however, this is his life and he doesn't know how much time he has left. Believing he will die because he has an expiration date is life-altering. He will be in a different mode of operation than anyone else.

The benefits for him are second-to-none:

- Extremely focused.
- Machine-like mannerisms to always be productive.
- Accomplish everything yesterday mentality. Meeting a goal's due date doesn't turn him on, but beating that date does.
- Very little will slow him down. Obstacles will just be inconveniences, and execution will continue, regardless of the challenges.
- Drama in his surroundings will be eliminated or managed appropriately.
- Extremely confident.
- He will get up with a purpose every morning. No

more lounging around in bed until the last possible moment.
- Always strategizing to be more efficient.
- Patience will be an ugly 4-letter word for him, but he will embrace it for mentoring others.
- Legacy minded.
- He will be happier because he's ultra productive and maintaining a balanced lifestyle.

Living life with a sense of urgency definitely has some incredible benefits, but if you don't live life with urgency, do you think your son will? The only potential drawback to living with urgency is that it may be difficult (at times) to stop and smell the roses. Excitement for accomplishments are second to none and are short-lived, maybe a few minutes and it's on to the next goal.

Hey, it's fun to play on Facebook or watch music videos for hours on YouTube, etc. It's one big giant playground that's open 24/7. That's a lot more entertaining than pursuing personal and professional goals. It's difficult to pull away and do something as boring as planning for your future. There's always tomorrow—right? This lack of urgency mindset is propagated throughout our society. Very few people live life with a sense of urgency. Time flies by, and a year later they haven't accomplished anything, and then five years zoom by with the same results. Help your son train his mind to use time wisely and abhor waste. Although the above process sounds morbid, it is not. Sure, I was fighting a major war on the inside to alter my lifestyle, but on the outside my happy-natured disposition remained the same. To learn more about how to live life with urgency, read my book titled *Live Like You Are Dying: Make Your Life Count Moment By Moment*.

Establish Phrases

Your son should choose phrases that are impactful and are easy to remember. I used phrases that were very negative to light that much needed fire under my butt. You can't get much more negative then: *I will die at 40*. I went for the gusto to help me get that extra edge (i.e., purpose, motivation, attitude, etc.). Just because I used negative phrases didn't mean I was a grouch. My personality was the complete opposite. I was always happy, cordial, and nice to everyone. On face value no one could tell I was using negativity to motivate myself. This method of training my mind was between me, myself, and I. Yup, there was a battle brewing daily to combat laziness or fatigue. It worked for me. My closest friend uses only positive affirmations to get that motivation and drive. No two people are alike. Help your son determine which phrases work best for him and make sure he consistently uses them until his mind is trained. I've provided a few phrases below.

Phrases to Help Redirect Negative Emotions

Example #1

I had a very difficult breakup in my late twenties. It was someone who I loved very much. When we separated, I was distraught. I lost focus, energy, and motivation. Within a few hours I was back to normal again because of a few very nasty phrases I said to myself repeatedly: *she's a loser, she's a piece of . . . She's probably with some other guy right now; she's not worth it . . .* In other words, I trashed her in my mind. Did I really feel that way? No way. However, my trained mind made me believe she was a bad person—that's all it took! The objective is not to look back and dwell on the past. It's over, put things behind you, and focus on the future. Life must go on—the sooner, the better.

Example #2

I had a close friend (at least I thought I did) who I treated like a brother. I provided him with continuous support (personal advice, business support, and financial help upon request). My friend had a lot of great qualities, but managing his finances effectively wasn't one of them. I lent him more than $100,000 over ten years. A promissory note was written and signed by both parties with each loan. In the end, the promissory notes were worthless. He never paid back a dollar—he defaulted on the loans.

A lawsuit ensued, and judgment was awarded to me. I was very upset and hurt—I couldn't believe that someone who I treated better than my own brother would burn me in this manner.

My trained mind redirected my negative emotions into my priorities by having me believe that he was a loser—it got me back on track quickly. I used phrases like: *he is nothing but a piece of . . . he's a loser . . .* Did I really feel this way about my close friend so quickly? Of course not. I still cared for him very much. I blamed myself too, because I knew about his financial management shortcomings. Regardless of how you feel, use key phrases that will get you angry enough to redirect those negative emotions into *powerful positive energy.* The key is to get back on track quickly.

I am happy to report that after several years of not speaking to my old friend, he reached out to me and began making amends— he sends me a percentage of his income every month. I forgave him—after all, we are all human and we all make mistakes. Our friendship continues to flourish.

Dealing with emotional conflict is probably one of the hardest challenges you will face. It is extremely difficult to hold yourself accountable when you are dealing with these sorts of setbacks. They are the biggest time wasters of all.

Make sure your son is prepared—bad situations WILL happen. When they do, he should know the phrases to use, and he should start repeating them over and over and over again until his mind takes over and leads him forward. Let's say he gets into a big fight with his significant other—he's in a bad mood, and he doesn't feel like doing anything.

He may want to try the phrases below to snap out of it:

- Precious minutes are being wasted—you're a fool to let this stupid fight drag on.
- The argument is over—stop dwelling on it—it gets you nowhere.
- You can't win—who cares who wins? It's irrelevant— give in—you have more important things to do.
- Step back and take a deep breath—do not be confrontational.
- She's a wonderful person—don't be stupid.

Repeating phrases to train the mind may sound a bit weird, but it's the best way to keep him on top of his goals. He needs to determine which phrases leave their mark and cause him to change, redirect, and stay focused on his priorities and milestones. Remember, his objective is to get on with his life as quickly as possible, not to wallow in depression.

Using negative phrases to redirect negative emotions may seem contradictory, but they are very effective. The nastier the situation, the more challenging it will be to train his mind. In these situations he needs hardcore methods to stay on track toward a more productive life.

On 10/12/15 I had written the note below to Alex. Her first love dumped her approximately three months earlier, and her goals were all put on the back burner. She wasn't moving forward, and it was affecting her future in a big way. Her emotions got the best of her, and she didn't know how to snap out of it.

Real Life Scenario: Getting Beyond Her First Love

"Hi, Love,

It's me again, dear old Daddy. Did I ever tell you how much I love you? I know how difficult it's been for you to get beyond Nick, your first true love. It's been several months now, and you're still distracted by his memories. Although you've been out with your friends and a few guys, you're still dwelling in the past—talking about him like he was in your life, and in many ways he is and he probably always will be. The fact that he left you makes absolutely no sense to you, and you're seeking some sort of closure. I understand that—believe me, I know—been there before several times. Unfortunately, that closure is not coming from Nick; it has to come from you. If not, you will still be in limbo for months to come, and you won't be able to focus on your goals. The best way to get closure is to play mind games by using negative phrases to train your mind. Once your mind has been trained, it will force closure. Your mind will convince you to move forward because it's trained to paint a different image of Nick. A very ugly picture to help Alex move forward. Whichever negative phrases have a bigger impact on you—use them. Thinking positively of him to date hasn't worked. I know this is difficult for you because you're such a kind-hearted person, but unfortunately it's the only way. I know you don't believe those horrible words, but it's a game that you're playing; however, you have to be a great actress and rehearse these lines over and over again to win. You must train your mind to believe that Nick is a piece of. . . and you're a better person without him. You have to play this game to win. Achieving success will allow you to get on with your life and focus 100% of your energies pursuing your goals. I know you don't want to hear any of this right now, but you need to move past this."

The next few days she actually made progress, and by the following week it seemed like she was back.

I asked her one day, "What did you do to get over him?"

"I trashed him in my mind like you taught me, and it worked. I also kept telling myself repeatedly that I was too good for him."

"Way to go, sweetheart, welcome back."

"Thanks, Daddy."

Be Repetitive, Play Mind Games

Mind games are phrases, routines, and actions your son should repeat over and over again until they're permanently entrenched in his mind and become part of his life. Silly as it may sound, playing mind games is the main ingredient to help him accomplish his goals.

His greatest ally, companion, confidante, etc., is and always will be his mind. Training his mind is best described as a series of premeditated steps that he takes to evoke a desired behavior. Whereas you train a muscle to perform a desired movement or motion, you train the mind to obtain desired concentration and attitude, as well as to defeat laziness.

It's difficult to remain motivated *every* day of the year. The only way is to convince your son to train his mind to push his body. Once he does that, he will consistently hold himself accountable and be successful in all his endeavors. Motivation will constantly nudge him forward even when he's tired and feeling lazy.

How to Stop the Procrastination— Permanently

"Time is the scarcest resource, and unless it is managed, nothing else can be managed."

—Peter F. Drucker

Peter Drucker hit the nail right on the head. How many people do you know of that manage their life? Very few. Did you ever stop to think why people always run out of time at the end of the day? Rarely do they get everything done for any given day. Time must be managed to get as many things done as possible. Without a doubt time is your most valuable resource. If your son is like most teens, he can't manage time effectively. The fact is (based on hundreds of personal and professional evaluations) procrastination and overall time management are the number one problem (by far) with adults and adolescents.

"You may delay, but time will not."

—Benjamin Franklin

Below is a simple process flow depicting four methods you can teach your son to master time. For him to be ultra efficient, all four methods should be utilized.

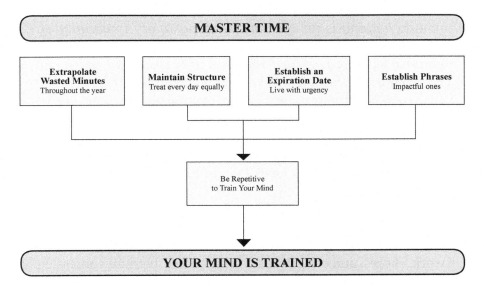

Below are some of the discussions I had with Alex to improve her overall time management.

Real Life Scenario: Mastering Time—A Huge Benefit

Alex used to say to me, "So what if I wasted a few hours today? I'm still young—there's always tomorrow, I have plenty of time."

"Alex, you should never look at lost time in minutes, hours, or days. Assess the average time you waste in a day, and extrapolate that throughout the year. You will have a rude awakening, love."

"I'm not sure how much time I waste every day."

"Let's just say it's four hours a day; I think it's more, but let's leave it at four to give you the benefit of the doubt. If I extrapolate four hours a day for 365 days, you're flushing two months out of the year from your life down the toilet. In other words, you would only be living ten months a year instead of twelve."

"OMG, I can't believe it."

"If that's not a sticker shock, I don't know what is."

"So let me ask you, when you're 21, you're still young—right?"

"Yes, I am."

"So when you're 25, you're still young—right?"

"Okay, you're right, Daddy. That's the wrong way to think about time."

"Time is precious, sweetheart; it's a sacred gift. Every day you do nothing is another missed opportunity to accomplish something wonderful. There are only so many chances in life. If you really want to put forth the effort to be successful, and it will be an effort, it's hard work. You witness how hard I work every day—you see it first hand. I'm sure on many occasions you've told yourself, 'I never want to work that hard.'

"You don't have to, but as you get older, you may want to, as well for the love of your family and for your profession. That's up to you. I do it for the love of my family—you, not to mention I like what I do."

"That makes sense, Daddy, thank you."

By far the number one excuse Alex uses with me is that she doesn't have enough time on any given day to complete her studies, work, chores, and obligations. I beg to differ, because witnessing her mode of operation paints a totally different picture.

I actually monitored her closely for one week and produced a similar list. When I confronted her and broke down the average time utilized for each category, she didn't argue; she just gave me a smirk. How much time can you afford to let your son throw away?

Imagine. . . .

There is a bank that credits his account each morning with $86,400. It carries over no balance from day to day. Every evening deletes whatever part of the balance he failed to use during the day. What would you do? Draw out all of it, of course!

Each of us has such a bank. Its name is time. Every morning, it credits him with 86,400 seconds. Every night it writes off as lost whatever of this he has failed to invest to good purpose. It carries over no balance. It allows no overdraft protection. Each day it opens a new account for him. Each night it burns the remains of the day. If he fails to use the day's deposits, the loss is his. There is no going back. There is no drawing against the "tomorrow." He must live in the present on today's deposits. Invest it so as to get from it the utmost in health, happiness, and success! The clock is running. He needs to make the most of today.

> *To realize the value of ONE YEAR,*
> *ask a student who failed a grade.*

> *To realize the value of ONE MONTH,*
> *ask a mother who gave birth to a premature baby.*

> *To realize the value of ONE WEEK,*
> *ask the editor of a weekly newspaper.*

> *To realize the value of ONE HOUR,*
> *ask the lovers who are waiting to meet.*

> *To realize the value of ONE MINUTE,*
> *ask a person who missed the train.*

> *To realize the value of ONE SECOND,*
> *ask a person who just avoided an accident.*

> *To realize the value of ONE MILLISECOND,*
> *ask the person who won a silver medal in the Olympics.*

Teach your son to treasure every moment that he has! And remember that time waits for no one. Yesterday is history. Tomorrow is a mystery. Today is a gift. That's why it's called the present!

"Lost wealth may be replaced by industry, lost knowledge by study, lost health by temperature or medicine, but lost time is gone forever."

—Samuel Smiles

Here are some areas where your son could be wasting time:

- Texting insatiably
- Surfing the Internet
- Always on social media
- Looking for something in his messy room
- Having all of his attention stuck on something upsetting that happened at school or work without doing anything to eradicate the situation
- Playing video games online with his virtual friends for long periods of time
- Having insignificant and long conversations with people
- Looking for clothes to wear each morning because he didn't pick out his clothes the night before
- Watching too much TV
- Daydreaming
- Reading inspirational quotes for hours
- Head buried in cellular

I probably missed some, but I think you're getting the picture. One evening when I picked Alex up from work. she brought up the subject of inspirational quotes as tattoos to help her get motivated and to be more productive. Below is that conversation.

Real Life Scenario: Inspirational Quotes as Tattoos to Combat Laziness—Really?

"Daddy, you know how much I love tattoos. I've decided to get an inspirational quote; maybe it will help with my laziness."

Oh, my poor aching head. . . but I just kept quiet that evening, and a few days later I began writing this response for us to discuss...

Dear Alex,

I love inspirational quotes, too; who doesn't? Actually, if you look in the back of the second self-help book I wrote titled Discipline: Training The Mind To Manage Your Life, *there are several pages of my all-time favorite inspirational quotes. There are also thousands of them on the Internet. They're fun to read, and some do motivate people, but unfortunately the inspiration only lasts for a few seconds or minutes, and then it's back to business as usual: being lazy.*

Over the years you've spent hundreds of hours researching and reading inspirational quotes to help you get motivated— right? Has it worked? The answer is no. You feel the adrenalin rush for a bit, but then it's back to being unproductive. You have a **serious** *issue, and putting an inspirational quote in the form of a tattoo on your body and reading it occasionally will not fix this problem. If that was the fix-all/cure-all, I would be the first one to tell you to do it, but nothing comes that easy in life. Anything fulfilling comes with a price. It's time to be a realist and do something to eliminate this very nasty characteristic that depicts who you are. Do you really want people saying you're lazy for the rest of your life?*

You can read a new quote every day, every hour, or even every few minutes. . . but inspirational quotes will NOT fix your laziness. The only thing you can do is train your mind to manage your life. Before I take the time to explain myself further, let me know if you want help. If so, I will gladly help you combat your laziness; if not, you know I will always love you.

Daddy.

I actually thought she was going to blow me off again, but she said, *"Okay, you're right. I need your help. I need to change— nothing is working."*

Below is another note I wrote a few days later:

Dear Alex,

We've discussed your laziness for months now. The only way to destroy this bad habit of yours once and for all is to play mind games and train your mind by utilizing the four methods we've discussed earlier. You also have to be a willing participant and want to fix this situation once and for all.

Using negative phrases

Let's come up with a few hardcore negative phrases that depict the true image of who you really are, Alex—a very lazy person. Phrases that will instill a sense of urgency, phrases that will make you jump to action. Instead of using positive phrases and inspirational quotes that sugarcoat this nasty problem you've had for years, use a few hardcore phrases that will cause change.

For example, if I was in your shoes I would use the following phrases:

- *I am lazy, pathetic and worthless. How long do I want to exist like this?*
- *Is this the role model I want to be for my children?*
- *I haven't accomplished a damn thing. Is this the way I want to live the rest of my life?*

Sure, these phrases are negative, and we've always been taught to think in a positive manner—and you should; however, thinking positive and facing the truth are two different things. You need to be brutally honest with yourself—not live in a fantasy world (i.e., fat is NOT beautiful) and certainly NOT healthy. Face the facts—face the writing on the wall. Why sugarcoat the fact that you're lazy?

Once you come up with your own phrases, repeat them constantly—every day! Eventually your mind will be trained. Once your mind is trained, you won't need to research for new inspirational quotes. Your mind will keep you motivated automatically and will keep you focused on your priorities, goals, and milestones 24/7. It's like being in boot camp and having your own personal drill sergeant attached to your hip. Good luck trying to be lazy—once your mind is trained, your personal drill sergeant (your newly trained mind) will give you that kick in the butt you were looking for with those inspirational quotes.

Treating every day equally to maintain structure

We have to establish an efficient morning and evening routine for you, too. Something simple that will enable you to treat every day equally. Treating every day equally means doing something consistently until it becomes habitual. Do the same thing every day with some modifications (i.e., work emergency, holidays, weekend schedule vs. weekday). Don't just live life by the seat of your pants—plan it out thoroughly. Be productive with your time and utilize every minute, then you can feel totally free to goof off and relax, have fun.

I can hear your internal flack now, Alex: "That's utterly ridiculous; there's more to life than just thinking about my routine and to-do list," or "Does that mean I have to be robotic-like all the time?" or "I can think about what I want to think about!"

These are all protests from your mind fighting the control. Your mind is used to having no control, sort of like a spoiled child. So, of course, it is going to give you a hard time and try to throw you off. All I'm saying is to take control of your mind and energy so that you are making progress on being productive every single day, whether it's painting, studying, or spending quality time with your family. The payoff will be that you accomplish a lot and stop flushing your life down the toilet. You are the captain of your ship. It is your life, so you should control the direction in which it goes—take control of your life. Once you learn that you can achieve your goals, then you are empowered to achieve higher levels of success and fun.

"Is this making sense yet?"

"Yes."

"It is so easy to get overwhelmed with all the distractions, especially with your cellular, that you can wind up going with the flow. However, the consequences of going with the flow, being pushed around by outside forces is that you never live your life, never accomplish your goals and end up feeling very dissatisfied and labeling yourself lazy for the rest of your life, and believe me, if you don't fix yourself now, it will be much worse to deal with this as you get older and are even more stubborn."

Set an expiration date so you can live like you are dying

"God forbid, but if you were diagnosed with a horrible disease that was terminal and the doctor told you that you had one year to live—what would Alex do? It sounds morbid, but you have a serious problem and you need to do something differently. I bet without warning, the lazy devil inside of you would be squashed. It worked for me, but whatever date you pick as your expiration, believe it truly is your final day on this planet."

To summarize into a few key takeaways:

- Be truthful with yourself, don't sugarcoat the problem
- Train your mind to combat laziness
- Productivity vs. laziness is like good versus evil. Evil will always try to trump good. If you don't train your mind, you will fail
- Inspirational quotes are fun to read, but will never fix your problem
- The problem will only get worse over time
- It takes a lot of effort to be ultra productive and zero effort to be lazy

"It's up to you, Alex; with the severity of this problem, I recommend you use all four methods to train your mind."

Over the next few months the new and improved Alex emerged. However, it wasn't always smooth sailing because old tendencies are hard to kill. There were some major setbacks along the way that impeded productivity.

One day I noticed that her laziness was rearing its ugly head again, waiting until the very last minute to get out of bed each morning instead of getting up to fulfill her morning responsibilities. At first it was just a few things; then after a few weeks she neglected all morning chores, including cleaning her room. I didn't realize how messy her room was until I had to go in there. It was the day that set me off in a major way. I made an appointment with a contractor to have some work done on our very expensive Plantation shutters. They were supposed to go into every room to make adjustments. We started in the library and then was heading into Alex's room, but as I opened the door, I took a quick look inside and was appalled by the scene. It was a disaster. It was so bad that I couldn't let the contractors into her room. We ended up bypassing her room. After they left, I went back up to take pictures. I was livid, because I couldn't believe that she let this happen, and besides I had to reschedule the shutter company to come out a second time just for her room. I kept quiet for a week.

I cooled down and mentioned that I wanted to talk. Below is that discussion.

Real Life Scenario: Laziness Finally Squashed

"Alex,
You know I manage my business from home, right?"
"Yes, I know that."
"What do you think would happen if I just lounged around in bed for an extra hour or two and took my sweet time about everything?"
"You probably wouldn't be as successful as you are today."
"I totally agree. You want to get your Real Estate license and start your own business, right? What would happen if you didn't push hard every day in the same manner that I push myself?"
She looked at me with those big sad eyes and said, "I wouldn't be very successful."
"Do you know why I am bringing all of this up?"
"Because I am being lazy again."
"Not only will this behavior affect your future, but it's impacting me in a very negative way, too. You're wasting my time, and for me time is precious and always has been."
"What do you mean, it's affecting you?"
"Look at these pictures of your room. I had people coming to work on all the shutters in the house last week, but I couldn't let them into your room. Do you see why?"
"Yes, sir," she said as she looked at me in an embarrassing manner.
"Effective today, you are on probation until further notice—for at least six months."
"What does that mean?"
"It means if you do not abide by your morning routine, I will forward these pictures to the love of your life."
"You can't do that; that's blackmail."

"Whatever you want to call it is fine. But this is for your own good. Either we nip this in the butt now, or your laziness will bite you where the sun doesn't shine. You can hate me now and forget about starting your own business or accept the punishment and fix it once and for all, therefore having a shot at success."

"Okay, Daddy, I'm sorry—let's beat it starting today."

I never had to send those disgusting pictures of her room to her boyfriend.

> *"Do more than is required. What is the distance*
> *between someone who achieves their goals*
> *consistently and those who spend their lives*
> *and careers merely following? The extra mile."*
>
> —Gary Ryan Blair

How Do you Hold Yourself Accountable: The End Result

Once your son's mind is trained he will:

- *Be in a continuous battle to improve*
  It's him against the man in the mirror and many obstacles—some bigger than others. Life is all about planning ahead for the inevitable and conquering those obstacles when they appear so he can eventually master every aspect of his life.

- *Redirect negative emotions*
  There will be plenty of negativity in his lifetime. He will be able to redirect that negativity into a positive force to help him stay focused and conquer his goals.

- *Live life with a sense of urgency*
  Time flies. The next thing he will realize is that he's thirty or forty years old. He looks back and asks himself, "What have I accomplished?" When his mind is trained to live with urgency, he will no longer procrastinate. He will be extremely focused on his priorities, obligations, goals, and milestones. He will want to accomplish everything before its actual due date.

- *Always be motivated*
- *Possess a never enough mentality*
  The more he accomplishes, the more he will want! He will never be satisfied!
- *Put pressure on himself*
  Life is full of stress and pressure. If he's prepared in advance for the unexpected and unrealistic (i.e., a project with an aggressive due date), he will succeed regardless of the challenge.

"I was always looking outside myself for strength and confidence, but it comes from within. It is there all the time

—Anna Freud

Being Disciplined

Once your son develops his self-discipline and is able to manage his life effectively, he will then reap the benefits of discipline. Being disciplined is a multifaceted and beautiful thing. First of all, it's an immediate reward in itself to see your son's face light up when he applies himself and realizes the impact it can have. Secondly, his life will be infinitely easier if you've mentored him with the principles highlighted throughout this book. Third, you need to do it for society. What do you want to contribute to civilization? A happy, well-adjusted young adult who contributes to it or one who struggles at every turn? If you want to give him every advantage in life to be successful, then make the effort to mentor him. Don't make the assumption that he will learn this knowledge from others, because the odds of that happening are pretty slim. It should come from you, but if another close family member or friend is willing, allow them to instill these ideas into his mind also over time. More role models are always better.

"Children have never been very good at listening to their elders, but they have never failed to imitate them."

—James Arthur Baldwin

The word success means something else to just about everyone. However, when people rattle off their definition, one connotation keeps reappearing in different terms: financial security. That alone is not enough to get Alex focused on her new adulthood priorities and to break that nasty addiction. Below I shared my definition of success in a manner that she could embrace and get excited about.

Real Life Scenario: Success is Only One Reward

"Alex, here are my definitions of success, and they're all of equal value: happiness (in my relationship with God, family, and your mom), career satisfaction, excellent health, growth in every area of my life, having so many accomplishments that I leave behind a legacy, and maintaining balance. Others measure it by money or material possessions, others by the number of rungs climbed up the corporate ladder. Do you know what made Daddy successful?"

"Yes, it's discipline; you wrote so many books on discipline."

"You're right, sweetheart. You've witnessed how mastering self-discipline has made me successful. For me, it's easy to relate success as the sole benefit of being disciplined. However, there is much more, and topping the list has to be its support when you're emotionally down, an aid to help you get back on your feet again. Life is challenging: half the time it's good, and half the time it's downright nasty."

"That's why having many friends isn't important," she quickly chimed in.

I was actually expecting that comment from her. "Sure, friends are important and great for sharing both the good and bad times, but they cannot always be there, especially as time passes and they have their own family issues to deal with. Second on the list has to be how being disciplined makes you a better all around person, excelling in personal and professional values."

"Being disciplined will also help when you have an injury. It will help you recover at an accelerated pace. No, it is not a magic healer, but it will keep you from feeling sorry for yourself, and it focuses your energy on positive thinking and accomplishing your goals! It's like your go–to person in football when you

desperately need a touchdown. Lastly comes success. Without a doubt, being disciplined will make you successful. Your career will take off, and so will your financial assets. Everything you touch will turn to gold. You will have an incredible appetite to achieve."

I rose to a different level—a level that allowed me to achieve more than I ever thought possible. I want the same for Alex.

Below is a summary of the benefits from being disciplined:

- Sincerity
- Ability to accomplish more than you ever thought possible
- Constant drive
- Perseverance
- Positive attitude to potentially help you heal faster from mental and physical injuries
- Courage
- Confidence
- Tenacity
- Resourcefulness
- Continuous thirst for knowledge
- Will and determination to succeed at anything
- Enthusiasm
- Energy
- Living life with urgency

Not a bad list of benefits! Just think how powerful these attributes are and what the potential would be for your son if he acquired these skills.

In the end, this book is about helping the most important people living on this planet: our children. As adults, we can have a huge positive impact on our children's future not only in the "time-tested" traditional way of being good disciplinarians, but also by preparing your son for adulthood by developing key life skills and a roadmap. The next section will focus on formalizing a time-tested action plan (roadmap), which I've coined the Personal and Professional Growth Program (P2GP).

Section III

Your Teen's Life, Inc.

Behind every successful business undertaking, there is a business plan that depicts how management intends to accomplish each objective. Sell this same principle to your son. He needs to manage his life as if it was a small business and his livelihood depended on its success. The more efficient he runs the company, the better the returns. If he manages himself effectively, the more productive he will be; therefore, the odds of his success are greatly improved.

Chapter 7

A Life Plan—
Introducing the P²GP

Section II of this book should spawn many action items for your son's development. It's important to compile a list of these tasks into a roadmap. In the professional realm I refer to it as a *Personal and Professional Growth Program (P²GP)*. It's the same process I used on Alex and for my life coaching clients.

It's content should include:

- A strategy going forward to combat his issues
- A detailed view and synopsis of his strengths and weaknesses
- Specific skills to develop with milestones
- A process to continuously gauge his progress
- A documented routine to follow, based on his priorities, goals, and milestones
- A process to ensure structure is maintained for efficiency

The P²GP will provide your son with a performance-enhancement roadmap of how to achieve results, add perspective to where to place focus within the goals he's established, and, most importantly, it helps to track daily milestones for which to accomplish his goals. It builds a framework for aligning professional goals and personal goals. The integration of goals is vital to becoming more productive.

Therefore, it can be determined if he is maturing and being productive. Is he meeting expectations? Is he waking up with a purpose? Is he living life with urgency? Is he communicating effectively with his colleagues and management? Is he structured and prepared to do great work?

There are four primary areas which become the premise for the P²GP:

1. *Dreams and vision*

    He has his dreams and a vision for a successful and happy life. For him to get from where he is today to fulfill his dreams takes planning, hard work, tenacity, and some urgency; otherwise, his dreams remain just that. The P²GP becomes the catalyst to reality. It's his strategy moving forward. Based on his strengths and weaknesses, what's the appropriate strategy to transition him from where he is today to that perfect life he desires?

2. *Self-discipline*
    Being disciplined is the greatest attribute he can acquire for success. Being proficient with his self-discipline will empower him to achieve almost anything; without it he will struggle to exist.

3. *Leadership*
    It's important to develop his leadership capabilities. Leadership skills can be taught and should be identified in the P²GP.

4. *Emotional Quotient (EQ)*
    EQ is his emotional intelligence, his interpersonal skills such as communication (written and verbal), managing emotions and relationships, just to name a few. EQ skills will have a greater impact on his life or business success than his IQ ever will. Due to the amount of time teens have spent in their virtual world, critical EQ skills have not been developed

properly. From studies, it has been found that those with a high Emotional Intelligence (EQ) are the happiest and get the most done. Up to a few decades ago, emotional intelligence was not even considered a factor in success. Emotional intelligence includes being able to recognize your own emotions and their triggers and learning to articulate them in such a way that is respectful of others' emotions. There are three categories that your son needs to focus on:

- *Self-management*
    ◦ Manage emotions and adapt to changing situations
    ◦ Motivation
    ◦ Redirecting emotions to avoid conflicts

- *Self Awareness*
    ◦ Is cognizant of his emotions
    ◦ Recognizes impact of his emotions
    ◦ Making sound decisions based on emotions

- *Relationship Management*
    ◦ Managing conflict
    ◦ Effective communication practices
    ◦ Influencing others
    ◦ Developing others
    ◦ Inspiring others
    ◦ Coaching others

EQ begins with your son and branches out to others he is involved with. It requires understanding, self-control, responsibility, and optimism. Some of its rewards are the increased ability to influence, communicate with, and inspire others. Can you see how your son's EQ directly influences his bottom line? Emotional intelligence is based on developing virtues and building character. It is based on his attitude toward others and toward himself.

** A special note to my readers**

If you're interested in receiving a free copy of the P²GP please email me at: harris@harriskern.com.

Mentorship

"There comes that mysterious meeting in your life when someone acknowledges who we are and what we can be by igniting the circuits of our highest potential."

—Mahatma Gandhi

The P²GP is an excellent time-tested process (utilized for over 10 years); however, without someone who is passionate about helping our teens succeed, it's just another process. Being a mentor is a special commitment. I will never forget my special mentor who changed my life five decades ago.

My neighbor Jim Jarman was in his forties when he made a deep impact on my life at age thirteen. Talk about a male specimen: intelligent, handsome, sincere, great physique, hard worker, good family man, and a great personality to match. I always looked up to him.

On one of those typical warm summer California days, Jim was outside mowing the lawn shirtless. We would always be clowning around together, trading sarcasm punches. On this particular day, he said the five magic words to me that changed my life forever: "Harris, you look like shit." As you can imagine, we were pretty good friends.

I could tell immediately that he was serious. He was right; I knew it. At the time, I stood six feet two inches tall and weighed approximately one hundred thirty-five pounds. If I turned sideways, you wouldn't be able to see me. I was that skinny. It was a disgusting sight!

I looked at Jim and said, "I know it, but I don't know what to do about it, and you know, I eat everything in sight, but I never gain a pound."

"Harris," he said, "Eating massive amounts of junk food is not the way to approach your problem. Your mind and body need a major overhaul, and it doesn't start with your mouth."

At thirteen, I did not understand what he was trying to tell me. "But how else do I gain weight?"

"If you decide to follow my instructions to the letter, then I will help you out."

I said, "Sure," not having a clue as to what was forthcoming.

"I want you here every Monday, Wednesday, and Friday after school. What time do you usually get home?"

"I get home at three each day," I replied.

"Okay, on those three days, I want you at my house by three-fifteen, and don't be a minute late. If you're late, the deal is off—no second chances." This was Saturday, so we started that Monday.

I was really looking forward to my first session. Maybe, just maybe, I could obtain a body like his in no time, and my life would change for the better. What a rude awakening! He put me through hell! To say it was a very stern exercise program is putting it mildly. It turned out to be three grueling days a week of torture, always pushing me harder than the week before. There was weight training, running, swimming (he taught me how to swim), and most importantly, lecturing me as we were exercising. He would always keep me focused on the exercise and our long-term objective. It was continuous badgering. There was no time or place for social talk.

Jim also went on to teach me not to rely on anyone for help. Why not? Is it not okay to rely on your friends occasionally? Not to accomplish your goals. It is 100 percent you and no one else. Athletes know that 80 percent is upstairs (in the mind), where it all starts, especially on those days that you're too tired, stressed out, or simply not in the mood––that's when you need to push yourself the most. He was training my mind more than my body, although I did not know it at the time.

Jim was like a drill sergeant. But the whole time, he was instilling me with key adulthood skills. I figured if he was willing to give up his precious time to help me out, the least I could do was show up on time. Besides, after I agreed to do this, he actually dared me to quit or show up late. He tested me during each and every one of our training sessions.

Looking back now, I realize what an illusory mind game this entire ordeal was. His tactics were highly effective. Now at the age of 62 and with a long list of accomplishments, I thank Jesus Christ, my parents, and Jim!

Chapter 8

Be a Mentor

"A leader takes people where they want to go.
A great leader takes people where they don't necessarily
want to go, but ought to be."

—Rosalyn Carter

We all know that being a parent is demanding and stressful, but being both a parent and a mentor truly takes a unique individual. My definition of a mentor is someone who is a leader, a visionary, has tenacity, and most importantly has the compassion, desire, and determination to see their teen accomplish their goals and do whatever it takes to help them succeed.

A mentor is not a disciplinarian or decision maker. Instead, a mentor echoes the positive values and cultural heritage parents and guardians are teaching. Below are the characteristics of a good mentor.

Leadership skills

When you speak, people listen and follow. You're a visionary with excellent EQ skills. Use your wisdom and strength to unlock the talent in your son. If you've been lucky enough to experience being mentored or having a coach, guide, or guru, then you understand the transformative power of having a true teacher. By this I mean a generous, wise, and experienced person, someone who's "been there" and is interested in their daughter's welfare and success. Leaders who are able to mentor, inspire, and actualize others have it within their power to also create high-performance environments.

A mentor should be a strong, assertive role model with a very positive and confident attitude. The mentor's demeanor is being watched closely and many times emulated by your children. Without a doubt the most important role models are parents. They are icons—idols even! Don't expect your son to come right out and say this because he won't; it's not the cool thing to do. But don't throw away this great opportunity to make a huge difference in his life. Parents aren't the only role models. Teachers, policemen, and coaches can also be considered secondary role models. Any one of these individuals can truly make a difference. Coaches do a wonderful job of disciplining our youth to excel in sports and acquire the required mental toughness. However, in my opinion, many of these individuals can do a better job of looking like role models. In respect to their physical appearance, many coaches are out of shape, and some are grossly overweight. I personally think this sends a terrible message to our youth who idolize, respect, and often emulate their coaches.

Communication skills

You must communicate effectively and persuasively to be a successful mentor. The overall approach must have a positive impact on your son. Ask questions—listen to what he has to say. Don't second-guess yourself. Ensure that both of you are on the same page at all times.

> *"The most important thing in communication*
> *is to hear what isn't being said."*
> —Peter Drucker

You need to establish the sort of relationship that will allow him to say what he wants when he wants. The goal is to get the relationship to the point where conversations never have to be sugarcoated. In other words, when you suspect something's not exactly right, you need to have the type of relationship where you can share your hunches or suspicions.

You will help your son strengthen his communication skills and educate him on how to relate well to all kinds of people. To do so, you should have exceptional communication skills and know how to balance between passive and aggressive message delivery. You must also communicate in a clear, direct, and sometimes a stern voice.

Sometimes he will say he understands, but he may not totally comprehend. It's better to over-communicate to be certain that he both comprehends and is comfortable with the direction and the task at hand. There will be occasions when you will need to persuade him that your approach is the appropriate route to take. Be able to negotiate.

"It's not what you say, it's what they hear that counts!"

—Don Shula

Negotiating skills

Good negotiating skills are a must when mentoring your son. Never try to force a solution on him, or he will probably rebel. When it appears that he isn't grasping the message, do not shove it down his throat. Be patient and persevere! Find other ways to articulate the message until you get the point across.

You must always portray confidence with the message, content, and approach during each discussion. If you lack mental firmness, he will know and may start to lose his confidence in your ability to mentor. Talk to him as if he is on the same playing field as you. Always treat him like an adult. These sessions are very important and are crucial to building a strong and trusting relationship.

Inquisitive

Go fishing. There will be instances when pertinent information is missing or not easily forthcoming from your son. Listen closely, ask questions, and read between the lines. His approach to soliciting feedback may not always be straightforward. You must scrutinize every detail to obtain the appropriate information.

"Listening, not imitation, may be the sincerest form of flattery. . . If you want to influence someone, listen to what he says. . . When he finishes talking, ask him about any points that you do not understand."

—Dr. Joyce Brothers, American Psychologist,
Television & Radio Personality

Persistent

There will be instances when you get frustrated with him. Perhaps he is not making progress or having a bad hair day. No matter what the barrier or how difficult the task at hand, never let up. Always look for creative solutions to move forward.

"Consider the postage stamp; its usefulness consists in the ability to stick to one thing until it gets there."

—Josh Billings

Inclination to help others

There is nothing more rewarding than helping him build the foundation to become successful in every aspect of life. He has to feel and see the sincerity and understanding from you throughout the mentoring process. He needs a caring adult who will listen to his aspirations and help him achieve those ambitions. Be genuine, be polite, respect his thoughts, and he will reciprocate!

Don't ever forget the stress, pain, and frustration you periodically went through as you were growing up. Be proactive; put yourself in his shoes to feel some of his emotional pain. It is essential to sympathize and truly understand his struggles and challenges. It isn't easy making plans for college, buying his first car, or planning for his future career. It has been proven that mentoring can improve his self-esteem by guaranteeing that someone cares and he is not alone in dealing with life's challenges.

✎ DID YOU KNOW

*About 40% of a teenager's waking hours
are spent without proper guidance and supervision.*

Patience

It's human nature to want results quickly, but it takes time to mentor a teen properly. Vital life skills aren't something that can be taught overnight. It typically takes months or even years. Be patient. Some days won't be easy. But nothing this worthwhile comes without a hefty price tag, a significant commitment, and a lot of time.

Positive outlook

It's important to always be energetic and positive. Your son needs to know that there will be bad days and good days, but on those really bad days, he needs to think of all the positive events in his life and not dwell on the negative.

I've had my share of negative events and expect plenty more of them in the future. When they occur, I quickly turn my attention toward *happy thoughts*: God, my wonderful kids, my wife, my health, my work, my daily exercise routine, or even my last vacation. My demeanor changes immediately. However, what works for me could be different for your son. It's important that he has his own happy thoughts and uses them to overcome negative situations at all times. If he's having a really bad day and those happy thoughts aren't changing his attitude, remind him that life is difficult, but the alternative is not an option!

> *"Keep moving if you love life, and keep your troubles well behind you."*
>
> —John McCain

Confidence

You must earn the trust and respect of your son. He needs someone he can turn to for advice. Think back to when you were young—did you always go to your parents to seek advice? Most of us were ashamed or embarrassed to discuss certain personal issues. Your son needs a confidante, a friend, someone he can trust—you, his mentor!

A moral code of conduct should be adhered to. Your son is

placing his very personal issues and challenges in your hands for resolution. Everything must remain confidential. Bottom line, you cannot be someone who enjoys gossip.

In an ideal world, most parents would be ecstatic if their son came to them for advice on personal and/or career issues. Unfortunately, this is not always the case. Many teens would rather discuss sensitive issues with their friends or schoolmates than with their parents. However, regardless of your current relationship (i.e., parent, neighbor, etc.), once both of you are on the same playing field and on the same team, your son will come to you first.

Uphold values

Values are guiding principles. They are the fundamental beliefs upon which all subsequent actions are based. Be honest, sincere, and caring at all times. Mentors do what is right, regardless of personal sacrifice.

A practitioner of self-discipline

If you're unproductive, procrastinate, and rarely accomplish your goals, don't bother mentoring someone else, especially your son. Is this the life you want for him? To reemphasize such a critical point, most teens will still not be prepared to take on the challenges of adulthood when they turn eighteen because our society doesn't provide enough guidance and mentoring for them. To state it bluntly, teens are being poorly prepared to handle the challenges of adulthood. All of us are continuously challenged to do more with less in our careers and personal lives. Your son will be faced with the same challenges, and you need to help him acquire the vital skills so he can successfully meet that challenge. You must step up to the plate and become mentors to give your son the ultimate gift—*arming him with the skills and the discipline to succeed.*

Keep it Simple

While helping teens develop adulthood skills, always keep the following in the forefront of your mind:

- Always try to broker a deal. Don't say "don't do this or don't do that." We all know that won't cut it with teens.
- Be articulate, but use simple words and sentences.
- Provide simple examples of how you would handle different scenarios. Always put yourself in their shoes. To date, it's been mostly all fun and games, and now you're helping them grow up and in a hurry.
- Don't try to cram too much into one coaching session. Bite off little chunks at a time.
- Be honest and don't sugarcoat anything, especially important discussions. Your son will appreciate it when you tell it like it is all the time. Honesty is always the best policy. Don't BS any discussion, regardless of how sensitive the issue may be.
- Provide details and plenty of examples.
- Treat them as an equal, not as a child.
- Communicate at an even keel demeanor, don't over-dramatize a point, but let them know that life is half good and the other half not so good. There will be just as many bad days as good days. The key is to learn from the bad days and continue to move forward, but teach them how to be prepared for the worst.

In Summary

It takes a special human being to become a Mentor. It's definitely not for everyone, as it consumes an enormous amount of precious time, and there are no monetary rewards. You're just helping your son transition to adulthood. There's nothing more!

To summarize the characteristics of a good mentor—someone who:

- Is an effective communicator
- Can negotiate

- Is inquisitive
- Is persistent
- Is patient
- Has a positive outlook
- Is a confidante
- Upholds personal values
- Is disciplined

. . . and most of all, someone who has a deep inclination to help others. To sum it up, mentors listen, feel, empathize, respond, and do whatever it takes to ensure success. Your son's future is in your hands. If you do it right, he'll excel. If not, the odds are quite high that he will struggle for the rest of his life.

> *"Leadership is not magnetic personality—that can just as well be a glib tongue. It is not making friends and influencing people – that is flattery. Leadership is lifting a person's vision to higher sights, the raising of a person's performance to a higher standard, the building*
>
> *of a personality beyond its normal limitations."*

—Peter Drucker, 1909, American Management Consultant, Author

Proactively Gauge Their Temperature

You need to constantly gauge your son's temperature. Proactively monitor his commitment to the program.

Keep your radar up and look out for these early warning signals:

- Diminished enthusiasm
- Frequent excuses
- Lack of results, i.e., missed due dates, inability to focus, etc.
- Personality changes
- Short or abrupt conversations
- Disrespectful behavior toward you
- Diversionary tactics

- A new goal that's "much more interesting"
- A personal crisis
- Content-free discussions. A sudden interest in abstract conversations
- Discussing unrelated issues

If these or similar symptoms occur, you must confront your son immediately to understand the underlying issues and resolve them as quickly as possible. If these problems are detected too late, things can get out of control and derail the entire mentoring program. You must pressure him to get back on track and complete what he set out to accomplish.

On any given day he may face stressful situations and difficult or unexpected decisions. Be proactive with him, and put all personal life challenges out on the table even if the issue sounds trivial. Regularly ask questions. If you don't, I guarantee he won't tell you what's troubling him, and one day you will be blindsided. At that point he's already crossed the line, and he may never be able to backtrack or recuperate.

Build Confidence Slowly

Success builds confidence. Once your son accomplishes a few simple goals, then he can take on bigger goals one at a time. Everything must be done in moderation, or your son risks failure. Make sure he doesn't try to take on the world (at least not just yet).

"The goal you set must be challenging. At the same time, it should be realistic and attainable, not impossible to reach. It should be challenging enough to make you stretch, but not so far that you break."

—Rick Hansen

The most effective way for your son to overcome many of his weaknesses is to build upon his strengths until he gains confidence. Once you see the light of confidence glow brighter, start to address his weaker areas.

Does your son have faith in his ability to make his dreams

a reality? Lack of faith in his abilities is a common first hurdle. A crisis of self-doubt can leave him on the sidelines of life wondering what would have been if only he could have mustered up the courage. He must give himself permission to believe that he is capable of a great deal more than he is allowing himself to believe. He should be willing to stretch himself and stretch his limits. He must be willing to overcome his insecurities and believe that he has what it takes to do what he wishes to do with his life and his talents.

But be careful of false pride or conceit. Believing that he is better than others will prevent him from lending a kind ear and from being compassionate, and this can come back to haunt him. Sooner or later, he will need a kind and compassionate ear, but if he has alienated those around him, then he will be out in the cold. Bragging about himself in order to show others that he is better is never a sign of true confidence or of positive self-esteem. He should believe in himself and in his abilities, but never at the expense of someone else's self-esteem. Mentor him to be a shining example of quiet self-confidence. The more he accomplishes in his personal and professional goals, the more confidence he will develop. Below is a discussion I had with Alex to accomplish as much as possible as quickly as possible.

Real Life Scenario: Life is All About Accomplishments

"Life has a practice of living you, if you don't live it."

—Philip Larkin

I asked Alex point blank one day when she was being way too lazy.

"Do you want to die having accomplished nothing or accomplish so much that you leave behind a legacy for your children like I am leaving for you, your mother, and brother?"

She looked at me with a straight face and said, "I'm just relaxing, and besides, I have plenty of time to finish my homework and chores."

"You've been sitting on that couch for over an hour, texting

with your friends. Finish your homework and all of your obligations, and then you can text until your fingers fall off. Responsibilities first, play time second. I don't think that's asking too much."

"Yes, sir."

"You need to realize that we're all on this planet for one time and one time only. There are no second chances, and our time is limited."

"I understand, Daddy""

"You do and you don't. You think because you're only eighteen, you have plenty of time, which is the wrong mentality. If you don't change your thinking when you turn nineteen, we will have this same conversation, and you will have accomplished very little. Time flies."

I continually ask myself: why are millions of people wasting so much time every day? I can't imagine not accomplishing one goal after another (major and minor) as quickly as possible until the day I drop. If there are no accomplishments, there is no life, or at best it's an unfulfilled life. There is no purpose for living. You may exist, but that's not living. Living is progressing, not merely breathing. Isn't this the mentality you want?

> *"To live is so startling,*
> *it leaves little time for anything else."*
>
> —Emily Dickinson

"Alex, there is no greater feeling in the world than accomplishing a major goal. Once you complete it, you will never forget that experience. It's hard to describe in mere words what the feeling is like. It's a kind of euphoria that not only makes you feel invincible, but it is extremely addictive as well. The level of intensity is relative to the difficulty of the goal. The harder the goal, the stronger the feeling of accomplishment will be. You can take my word for it."

"I still remember each and every goal, even the ones I accomplished over 40 years ago. There is no doubt in my mind that life is about accomplishments and feeling on top of the world each time you've achieved one. What a rush, one after another, like no other feeling. Those are real highs. It's a self-

inflicted adrenaline rush that you can't get out of your system once you've experienced it. The more you accomplish, the more you crave to achieve. You will never be satisfied. What a feeling it is to always want more and have that hunger to take on new challenges and to accomplish more year after year. Life now has purpose. Don't be complacent; don't waste valuable resources."

Living by Numbers

Alex is always telling me that she's bored when she's not hanging out or communicating with her friends. I am constantly telling her, "Sweetheart, make life challenging. We're here on this planet one time, and we don't know when our number will be called. So why not make the most of it?"

Teach your son to always grow in every aspect of life, but that's easier said than done. One of the best ways to do that is to teach him to associate a number with an activity or an important milestone. It's important that he knows his baseline numbers—his objective should be to always beat that number.

Below are some examples of how your son can beat his previous best number:

- If he allocated one hour to study for a previous math exam and he got an 84, he should allocate 1.5 hours of quality time when he's well rested to beat that number.
- If he works out at the gym and squatted 145 pounds last month, then he should try to squat at least 150 pounds this month. If he burned 250 calories on the elliptical machine today, then have him try to do 255 the next day.
- If he has one thousand dollars in his savings account, he should do everything possible to increase it to two thousand dollars.
- If he only prays a few days a week, make sure he puts it on his to-do list and consistently prays every day of the year.
- If he's earning two thousand dollars a month now,

help him assess alternative options to increase his income.

- If he's wasting 2 hours a day babbling and texting with his friends, then he should try to reduce it—preferably in half.
- If he currently snoozes past his phone alarm for twenty minutes each morning, he should try to reduce it to ten minutes and eventually zero.

I think you're getting the picture. Every area in his life can be measured, therefore, managed properly. "You can't manage something you can't measure." He should always challenge himself and outperform his previous best—isn't that what life is all about? Make life fun and challenging—grow!

Chapter 9

Maintain Balance—Sounds So Easy

My definition of having a rewarding life is one that is full of health, happiness, wisdom, success, and plenty of accomplishments to leave behind a legacy for your family. Simply stated, it's putting equal focus in the areas of your mental, physical, emotional, and spiritual well-being. Sounds like an easy goal, right? Maintaining balance will be one of the toughest challenges in your son's lifetime. Very few people can maintain a balanced lifestyle.

Spending too many cycles in any one area of life is a very common occurrence. I should know; I wrote a book titled *On Being a Workaholic: Using Balance and Discipline to Live a Better and More Efficient Life*. It's easy to get sucked into focusing on one area of your life like work, and everything else becomes secondary. Below are some additional commonly abused areas adolescents should know about.

These real life scenarios came directly from my life coaching engagements (using fictitious names):

- Mr. Jones reached out to me because he couldn't accomplish his goals. After an assessment I found out that he was spending a minimum of 10 hours a week helping his friend accomplish his goals. Nice gesture, but foolish in the end.

- Ms. Smith spent too much time on personal hygiene every day. Her daily shower actually lasted over one hour. Then another 1.5 hours on makeup and futzing around with her long hair. Approximately 2.5 hours each day—unreal! Other areas like her career suffered.

- Ms. Brown used to spend four hours a day in the gym. She wondered why she couldn't make her business and relationships work.

- Ms. Jordan spent several hours a day reading self-help propaganda for years, yet never accomplished her goals.

- Mr. Roberts spent several hours every day on spirituality. He excelled in that one area, but put his finances on the back burner until he lost everything and had to file for bankruptcy.

I think you're getting the picture. If your son spends too much time in any one area, then other areas will suffer. If he's not proactively doing something daily to promote balance, it will never happen. Balance is one of the most overly used words in the English dictionary. Below are some benefits of living a balanced lifestyle and the risk of existing in an unbalanced way of life.

The Benefits of Living a Balanced Lifestyle	The Risks of Living an Unbalanced Life
Good mental, spiritual, emotional, and physical health	Putting all of his eggs in one basket. His energy and focus are on one area of his life. If things don't go according to plan, it could destroy him, and then he's left with nothing
Improved personal life	Failing in his personal relationships. He won't have the resources to invest quality time for friends or other special people in his life
Enjoying vacations with his loved ones	If he's married, chances are he will go through a very painful divorce
Improved quality of life by focusing on career, health, relationships, and finances equally	Abandoning spirituality (always too busy)
Being happy and productive	Loneliness and depression—burying his head further into his work when there are critical emotional issues to deal with. His work or one other priority becomes his only outlet
Spending *quality* time with family or someone special consistently—even if it's only one hour a day	Living an unhealthy lifestyle
Preventing some of the risks from occurring when focusing on only one priority	
Reducing stress	

It won't be easy to achieve and even harder to maintain a more balanced way of life, but it's doable. Compulsive addiction takes time to develop, and it will take considerable time to overcome.

There's only one way to maintain a balanced lifestyle, and that's to make sure that obligations, tasks, and projects that are associated with priorities are in the forefront, written down on a to-do list daily. For example: taking out the garbage, picking up his brother from soccer practice, cleaning the toilets, reciting prayers, washing the car, working out, etc. All of these non work-related obligations should also be noted on his to-do list. Out of sight and out of mind apply big time to maintaining that balanced lifestyle. Help your son keep things front and center!

SECTION IV

The Roles of Technology in Education and the Family

Written by: Ina D'Aleo

Technology is a tool that can provide another way for children to learn and make sense of their world.

—George S. Morrison, Early Childhood Education Today

The Origin and Evolution of Technology

Technology has evolved for centuries, but since the advent of the Internet, it has advanced at a much faster clip, as if it was on steroids. This is why the goals of education and what it means to be scholarly these days are also changing quickly. For example, let's undertake literacy; in order to be considered educated today, students not only have to read, write, listen, and speak, but they also have to be savvy in technology. We call it *technologically literate*. Almost all children are tech savvy, beginning with toddlers who know how to navigate computer screens and use some apps on a tablet before they even get to conventional literacy skills like reading and writing.

Technology has made great advances in medicine, education, manufacturing, agriculture, just to name a few. There's no aspect of civilization that hasn't been touched by technology. Hi-tech inventions have made our lives diverse and exciting and brought us many conveniences. We don't even have to leave our home to order something; we just do it by the click of a button. In addition, through digital devices people now share their feelings and ideas. It's difficult to imagine how the world looked like centuries ago when technology was in its infancy.

The need for technology existed since the early years of mankind, as there was always a need to adopt new gadgets for living. The first technological inventions were mechanical tools like an arrow, plow, hammer, pencil; therefore, *technology* is not a new word as many might think. The word technology came from Greece and originated from the Greek word *techne*, which means "*art, craft, skill*" and logos, which stands for "*word and speech.*"

The need for art and speech still finds a place in our lives; we like to draw and design as well as speak and read, but through the years of technological advances, our skills have become more advanced and refined: besides using a pen to draw, we can also use graphics to design art digitally, and if we want to talk, read, and share our experiences with others, we would attend a podcast on the Internet.

Is Technology Good or Bad?

Not only is technology popular and widely used today, but it literally permeated our lives as well as the lives of our children by changing our viewpoint as well as our family dynamics. The biggest problem that our children face today is technology overuse, which causes a sedentary lifestyle and affects children's emotional and physical well-being. Many teenagers happen to be victims of the Internet by not being properly educated and supervised about online safety. Adults complain that parenting is harder today because technology limits their parental influence regardless of all the conveniences and choices that technology provides.

So is technology good or bad? Technology is neither good nor bad, but it's very powerful, and it's important to harness that force so it won't govern our time and our children's lives. What's the best way to do it? I believe that, *first*, parents shouldn't rush to introduce technology to their children at an early age, especially when they're still babies. Instead, they should introduce books with nice pictures and read to their toddlers whenever possible. *Second*, once you introduce your children to the "screen," you need to teach a balanced approach to technology by setting rules and time brackets from the very beginning. And *third*, parents need to be good role models themselves. They need to walk the talk instead of being constantly plugged into their gadgets. It's all about *moderation* and using common sense.

As adults we also trust in technology. As a mom and a teacher, I am a big supporter of technology, which I use daily. My favorite digital devices are a laptop, my primary source of information, a Kindle where I have plenty of books downloaded with access to them any time I please, and my cell phone that serves primarily as an important tool to connect with my son to ensure he is safe and well.

Let's have a better look at the role of technology in our children's lives by considering all the pros and cons and what we can do to help them stay connected safely.

What's the Right Age to Introduce Children to Technology?

Yes, kids love technology, but they also love Legos, scented markers, handstands, books, and mud puddles. It's all about balance.

—K.G., first-grade teacher

Technology has a great deal to offer today, and there is much that children can learn in all domains—cognitive, social, emotional, and linguistic. There is software that is designed for babies as young as 6 months old. It's often called *lapware*, because babies are held in their parents' laps to use it. Many parents think it's cute, and they really believe using software as early as six months will make their baby smart and give them a head start. Parents don't know that the later they introduce technology to their children, the less risk there exists for developing an addiction.

Most experts agree that it's better not to introduce devices to toddlers until they are two years old. This is the time when a child's brain goes through many changes, and children will benefit much more from interacting with adults or books read to them than accessing electronic devices. "Children under two years old learn best from real-world experiences and interactions, and each minute spent in front of a screen-based device is a minute when your child is not exploring the world and using their senses, which is extremely important in their development process," says Dr. Carolyn Jaynes, a learning designer for Leapfrog Enterprises. "However, by age three, many children are active media users and can benefit from electronic media with educational content. This content often uses strategies such as repeating an idea, presenting images and sounds that capture attention, and using a child rather than adult voices for the characters." (Brown, 2011).

Technology also plays an important role for teachers, how they instruct and how children learn. It is literally changing the world of education starting from an early childhood. Programs such as *Jumpstart Baby, Reader Rabbit, Playtime for Baby,* and many others are becoming more and more popular among parents. The most popular software *Leapfrog* is a curriculum-based program that teaches basic skills of reading, math, and science. The popularity of these programs is constantly growing (Morrison, 2011). As children get older, they continue to use technology in the classrooms as a study aid that helps them extend their knowledge base.

Utilizing Technology as a Way to Promote Social Development

Technology is just a tool. In terms of getting the kids working together and motivating them, the teacher is the most important.

—Bill Gates

How many times have we heard that using computers doesn't promote proper communication practices and hinders social development? I agree if utilized unsupervised; however, if it's planned appropriately and used properly, technology can support social development by improving communication. For some children who have difficulty communicating, computers and other tech devices are great methods for socializing with their peers in the classroom. Nothing can replace a real person when it comes to interaction, but for children who have serious speech disorders and still want to be a part of the classroom curriculum, technology serves as a link that connects classmates. Teachers who are technology friendly and like to integrate devices like computers or iPads in the classroom know how to accomplish these goals. One of the methods is teaming up students on projects, which encourages children to work together as a team and listen to each other. After the project is complete, children are encouraged to demonstrate their assignment and share information about their project to the class. In this scenario, technology is very helpful to students who are not motivated by traditional teaching methods.

When discussing the growth of technology and how quickly it changes, new opportunities to help in education are always available. Many schools have already adopted iPad technology in the classrooms, considering it a powerful tool for learning. Teachers and students love iPads because they're portable and load quickly, which gives them fast access to necessary information. The entire class can look at a classmate's work by attaching an iPad to the white board.

iPads are really helpful tools when it comes to learning, especially for researching words and definitions, but many teachers agree that iPads are only used as a supplementary tool; they don't replace the traditional method of learning by using paper, pencil, textbooks, and workbooks.

Technology as an Enabler for Children with Disabilities

When discussing technology in education, it's impossible not to mention the impact it has on children with special needs, including students with disabilities. *Assistive Technology*, which includes devices used to promote learning for students with disabilities, underwent drastic changes and contributed a great deal in helping children to make progress and build confidence in the classroom. For example, touch-screen computers and communication boards can assist students who have limited mobility and difficulty with communication.

One of the ways to assist children in communication is with the use of *Picture Exchange Communication System (PECS)*. This software is very helpful to those students who lack verbal skills and learn to express their thoughts by using pictures, which they select. This program is especially popular when working with students with autism and those who need help communicating and being more social. (Morrison, 2011).

Assistive technology helps children with visual impairments to see and helps children with physical disabilities to read, write, and be mobile. This changes their whole outlook on life, making the world around them more accessible and enjoyable.

It's important for teachers, including early childhood educators, to accept and use computers and technology in their classrooms and promote technological literacy, but at the same time the emphasis should be made on Internet safety with time limits on usage. Classroom technology is used to facilitate teacher-student collaboration, but it's only a study aid, and it will never replace a classroom teacher and teacher-student interaction.

Using Technology to Meet Different Learning Methods

We know that "one size doesn't fit all" in education. Children have their unique requirements and methods of learning, which is why educators developed specific techniques to meet the needs of students with disabilities. Technology is leveraged to help accommodate special needs: *Visual, Auditory, Tactile, and Kinesthetic*. Some children need to see, hear, touch, and others need to move in order to remember. Teachers can combine each learning style with a different type of technology or match different assignments with specialized software. For example, children who are visual learn better from objects like graphs, charts, and pictures. They like PowerPoint presentations for learning and processing new material. Auditory learners can retain information when they listen. Kinesthetic and tactile learners retain information best when they are touching, moving, and drawing. Students can interact with technology at their own pace, go back to the previous topics, and review material. The teacher establishes the atmosphere in the classroom and orchestrates the learning, but technology facilitates it and makes it more exciting and comprehensive.

Digital Natives and Digital Immigrants

Digital Natives and *Digital Immigrants* are the terms that were used and emphasized in the article "*Digital Natives, Digital Immigrants*" (2001) by Mark Prensky, an education consultant. He defines *digital* natives as the generation of people born during or after the rise of digital technology; in other words, these are our children, while *digital immigrants*—people born before the digital technology era—would be us parents and teachers. According to M. Prensky, new technology has changed the way today's students think and process information, making it difficult for them to respond to conventional ways of learning: children raised in a digital world would benefit more from media-rich learning environments by holding their attention and piquing their interest. Teachers should update their teaching techniques by turning to digital devices that they are less familiar with than their students. The article is pretty controversial, as it talks in favor of digital devices rather than traditional teaching techniques. Yes, teachers should update their method of teaching and they should keep up with technology, but many teachers would agree that they cannot turn completely to digital devices and miss out on real student-teacher interaction, which builds up trust and respect. Although parents may not be as tech savvy as their children, in most instances it shouldn't prevent them from participating and supervising their children's activities.

Technology as a Link between Parents and School

Parents are busy. They see their children in the morning before they send them to school and back in the evening when they come home from work. In many instances, when a school day is over, children are picked up by babysitters or school buses that take them to afterschool programs, which makes it challenging for parents to see their child's teacher to find out how they're progressing and which areas need improvement. But with the help of technology, parents now have a chance not only to communicate with their child's teacher, but also access the school's website and other school resources on line, which allows them to monitor their child's progress. Parents can access school accounts/links that provide them with the most updated information, including behavior, grades, and test scores, in other words, an ongoing record of a child's development. This online venue is a huge convenience for parents, which saves them a lot of time. And if they want to know more about their child's progress, the fastest and the most convenient way is emailing the teacher. Most teachers today prefer email as a way of communicating with parents.

As a teacher, I like to contact parents via email. Most of my students' parents work, and I don't have a chance to see them often, if at all, except those days when we have parent-teacher conferences. By emailing, I can inform them about their child's progress or my concerns. I also send pictures regarding trips and other events that occur in their child's school life. Parents like it, and it contributes to a good parent-teacher relationship.

Although, these are all advantages of technology, there are many disadvantages that dominate children's lives and make them struggle at school. When does technology become a disadvantage? How can we avoid it?

Not All Media Are Harmful

There are three discrete media categories (Pressman-Donaldson, Jackson, Pressman, 2014):

1. *Media consumption*: To use media passively, without contributing.
2. *Media creation*: To produce and distribute something in a way that requires active engagement, acquired skills, and complex problem solving.
3. *Media communication*: To use media to connect with another person.

We don't want to eliminate technology from our children's life, but we want to ensure they use technology as a useful learning tool, which will aid them to acquire the necessary skills for their education and future career.

With parental guidance technology can be used to our children's advantage by developing necessary skills like:

- Knowing how to create presentations using PowerPoint.
- Having a good command of Word Processing skills (it's not exactly the same as writing emails): spell check, table creation, working with headers and footers, text alignment, margins and line spacing, etc.
- Knowing how to use advanced search features that let children retrieve more information than a regular search engine.
- Basic Excel expertise that would allow children to use a spreadsheet to create a graph and paste it into a report.
- Digital drawing. There is graphics software for children that includes creativity tools for image creation and animation.
- Podcasting. A podcast is like a radio show, but instead of being broadcast live, it's recorded and then distributed over the Internet, and you can listen to it any time. Podcasting is a good way of allowing children to use their work and experience over the Internet.

Games, apps, and media are very addictive and powerful: they can take a hold of your children's lives by making them passive, lazy, irritated, making them lose interest in many other important things, or they can introduce them to a number of useful things by opening up new opportunities and ways of learning.

If your children are already into technical devices and are asking you for permission to play with them, then use those devices to their advantage, so they will learn and have fun at the same time. Don't forget to limit their screen time before you hand them a cellular phone or a tablet. There are a number of educational games that are available with a little research, or you can also use some from the list below that your child would enjoy. These apps will help your children with numbers and simple addition, letters, sounds, literacy, and creative drawing. They're appropriate for children ages 2-6. Be aware that how your child learns and processes information depends on their age as well as their potential; therefore, go through these games together, and if for some reason your child finds it hard or challenging, move on to a less difficult one. Children shouldn't get frustrated over doing something that isn't age appropriate or difficult. They need to learn by being able to understand and perform tasks, and only when you see your child is comfortable with navigating through and accomplishing tasks, move on to a more challenging level. Make sure that whatever games your children are playing, they foster their curiosity, build concepts, and provide learning beyond play.

Below is a list of educational apps, which can be downloaded on their devices:

- Avokiddo ABC Ride (iPhone, iPad)
- Barefoot Word Atlas (iPhone, iPad)
- Beck & Boo by Avakiddo (iPhone)
- Bugs and Buttons (iPhone)
- Busy Shapes (iPhone, iPad)
- Color a Draw for Kids (Android Phone, Kindle Fire)
- Dragon Box Algebra (iPhone, iPad, Android Phone)
- Dr. Panda and Toto's Tree House (iPhone, iPad, Android Phone, Kindle Fire)
- Hoopa City (iPhone, iPad, Android Phone, Kindle Fire)
- Kids ABC Phonics (Kindle Fire)
- Kids Numbers and Math (Kindle Fire)

- Letter School (iPhone)
- Reading Rainbow (iPad)
- Rosetta Stone Kids Lingo Word Builder (iPhone, iPad, Android Phone, Kindle Fire)
- Starfall Learn to Read (Android Phone)
- Super Why ABC Adventures: Alphabet (Kindle Fire)
- Toca Town (iPhone, iPad, Android Phone, Kindle Fire)
- The Cat in the Hat (Android Phone, Kindle Fire)

For more games and apps including those that can be used by older children, go to www.commonsensemedia.org.

Some of you are too busy to sit down and teach your children even the basics like counting or the alphabet—they prefer to have their child learn with the help of a tablet or computer, taking into consideration that it's entertaining at the same time. Don't blame yourself, especially if you are very busy. The time children spend with you is the most precious and not neccesserily in terms of conventional learning (i.e., "Let's sit down and count to fifty"), but in terms of bonding, building up trust, and learning important values. However, if the reality is that you can only attend to your child's basic needs and don't have time for anything else, then the use of these devices is extremely helpful when it comes to your child's learning. I see it as an option, as long as it's educational software with time limitations.

The Internet or Real Books

A big advantage of the Internet is that it can serve as a study aid for school children without the need of going to the library and spending hours scanning through different books to find information. Going online and using search engines like Google saves time finding resources and makes homework more enjoyable and easier to complete. However, when children get older and undertake more serious studies, the Internet alone is not enough.

Going to the library or bookstore and using books becomes a priority for many reasons:

- Even though Internet resources are available 24/7, the information is more concise in comparison to what children can find reading books, especially if they need to prepare for exams.
- Even if you find a good source for information on the Internet, your access can be very limited just like the content you are seeking, and you will still have to refer to books or magazines.
- Not everything on the Internet is free. Sometimes you only have access to some information, and if you want to read more, you need to pay or subscribe.
- Another disadvantage of the Internet is that the material is not well organized, and quite often you have to expend a lot of time to find what you are really seeking.
- Unfortunately, there's no quality control on the Internet. There's a lot of junk, misconceptions, confusing information. Anybody nowadays can create a website or post any information they want. You have to be careful when you read something and use your own judgment about how much you can trust the content. Books in the stores and libraries go through editors and fact checkers that make information more reliable and complete.
- When you are in the library, you deal and rely on people (librarians) who help you find what you need. You can get a good piece of advice and find what you're really searching for without spending hours going through different online resources.

Nothing will replace a library or bookstore, especially to those who love books and consider themselves avid readers. I love my Kindle because I can purchase a book and read it right away without going to a book store, but even I admit that regardless of the convenience, I still prefer an old fashioned book that allows me to touch and feel pages and even smell the print, especially if a book is new.

Parents and teachers always encourage children to read more. If your son or daughter finds a device interesting and engaging and it promotes reading at the same time, then let them use it to their advantage. But don't forget the importance of introducing your children to libraries and bookstores.

It is so crucial for us parents to guide and encourage our children through their childhood and teen years to make the right choices. Our goal is not to remove technology from their life, but to show them how it can be used as an asset that will improve their quality of life.

The Dangers of Technology

I fear the day that technology will surpass our human interaction. The world will have a generation of idiots.

—Albert Einstein

If you have a teenager, how would you describe their day after school or on the weekend? Playing computer games? Text messaging? Watching YouTube? Spending hours on PlayStation? More likely yes to one or several of these activities. I know, because I have a twelve year-old son who would spend countless hours on computer games and other electronic gadgets unless I set limits and constantly remind him about his priorities. Besides not being productive, excessive usage also changes a child's personality by making him or her zombie-like and easily agitated if interrupted while playing.

Children ages five through their teenage years are seriously glued to their screens. Most of them today can't separate themselves from their cell phones and computers. Do you see these children on the streets with their ears glued to their mobile devices every day, doing nothing but playing computer games? It's called addiction.

According to Nicole Stevens, the author of *Too Much Technology May Harm Children*, a new study shows that children may even exhibit withdrawal symptoms similar to drug addiction if they don't get their technology fix. In fact, some children have become so dependent on entertainment that they're considered clinically addicted. Besides the old traditional methods of playing with their peers, children can interact via computer games in a unique way. They live in their world, a virtual world that distances them from the real one. This is very detrimental to children, as it affects their performance at school and their grades.

Entire generations seem to be growing up addicted to technology. Food is left uneaten, homework is not done or incomplete, and sleep is lost. Technology at home is used as a pacifier for children because it keeps them occupied so parents can take care of their own things, although parents don't like to admit it. Most parents know that their children spend too much time playing games, watching TV, or text messaging, but they don't do anything about helping them occupy their time in a healthier matter in addition to not spending adequate quality time. Yes, they enjoy the entertainment and they are happy, but all this encourages passive enjoyment that's getting worse with time. Once children are addicted to technology, video games, and social media, they want more.

Eventually, kids get so lazy that they choose to spend a nice day inside the house glued to their screens rather than go out and enjoy the beautiful weather. It's sad that being connected to their devices gets them disconnected from the real world.

Technology without limitations also affects children's health: staring at the screen for many hours is detrimental to their vision. According to the American Optometric Association, lots of children have what's called *Computer Vision Syndrome*— eye focusing problems, eye irritation, fatigue, and blurriness. Other problems include neck pain and poor posture, which are also affected by being constantly engrossed in video games and looking down into their cellular devices. All these issues can be very damaging if not addressed properly and promptly.

Advice for Parents

First of all, you need to admit that your child is addicted. Don't say, "This is what all children do nowadays." You know they're addicted, some children more than others.

Below are some tips for parents:

- *Set rules for playing games*
  If one of your guidelines is for your child to play a maximum of 2 hours and only if their homework is

done, make sure they don't rush and complete their assignments haphazardly or not finish them at all. Be firm with the number of playtime hours you give your child. If they start objecting by saying that it's not fair, just say, "One hour or zero."

- *Get involved with their homework*
  Make time and check your child's homework. Yes, it's time consuming, and it may be even hard to do especially if they're in high school, as you may not be familiar with the course material; however, by looking through their assignments, you will still have an idea of how well and neatly they've completed it. You can always read through their writing assignments like essays or projects and see if they put forth their best effort. If their homework looks sloppy, then you know that you have to take away their screen time (i.e., computer, TV, or PlayStation). Make it clear that homework is their priority, and they cannot proceed to leisure activities until they do superior work. It disciplines them and imposes good study habits, and eventually this will lead to good work habits by teaching them to adhere to their priorities. I am not a big fan of allowing my son to use his computer or PlayStation during school days because I know that he will rush through his homework. I allow him to use his computer on a school day occasionally and only as a reward or, if for some reason, he doesn't have any homework. He uses his computer only on weekends provided that he is already finished or almost done with his homework for the upcoming week.

- *Establish a written contract*
  Some experts suggest that you should come up with a written contract where you write down the rules, let your kids read them, discuss them, and agree to them by signing the contract. The most important thing that you as a parent can do is consistently make sure your child is adhering to this contract.

- *Eat dinner with your children*
  Establish a family ritual to eat dinner together and make sure your children don't bring their cell phones to the table. Eating dinner jointly allows them to interact with you and be more involved in family-related conversations. Try not to turn on the TV while you're eating, regardless of how tempting it is, especially if you have the TV in your kitchen. Enjoying quality dinner time without electronic distractions is much more calming and beneficial for your conversations. According to the research highlighted in the book *The Learning Habit* by S. Donaldson-Pressman and R. Jackson, children who eat dinner with their parents play 50% fewer media games.

- *There are many opportunities to spend quality time with your children*
  If you spend time in the kitchen fixing dinner, you can ask them to do their homework at the dining table instead of in their room where they keep all of their devices. This way, they have fewer distractions. How many times did they tell you that they were going to their room to do homework, and half an hour later you see them logged into their computer and doing something else? It's hard to keep them focused and restrain them from checking social media sites like Facebook, Twitter, Instagram. . .

- *Get them involved in some sort of physical activity*
  Enroll them in at least one sport or at your gym. Because of passive media consumption, many children today are not physically active, out of shape, and growing up to be real klutzes.

- *Keep track of your child's progress in school by communicating with the teacher*
  If you find out that your child is not focused, distracted, is not making progress, or even worse—regressing, then something needs to change. If you know that your son or daughter needs to put more effort into studying and spend less time on

unnecessary stuff, then computer time should be very limited if not removed altogether until you see academic improvement. Please don't take away extra activities from your child as some parents do. Besides going to school, children need extra activities to develop and grow, especially if they enjoy them. Either it's playing soccer, tap dancing or chess—all of these contribute to personal growth, improved social skills, and building confidence.

- *Don't compromise chores*
  If your children are old enough to do some chores around the house: cleaning up their room, washing dishes, watering flowers, cleaning up after a pet. . . let them fulfill their obligations before they have their screen time. Be consistent with the chores; don't compromise. If your child's room is a mess or the cat's litter box is not cleaned up yet, then make sure they put away their tech devices and do their chores.

- *Try not going to bed before your kids*
  Don't leave them alone in their room with their devices. Whether they're playing games, watching YouTube, or chatting with their peers, you never know what they're going to do once you're asleep. Be overly cautious.

- *Cellular phones should be off before going to sleep*
  Make sure your children either shut down or silence their cell phones before going to sleep or leave them in a different room so their sleep is not interrupted by a phone call or texting.

- *Don't put a TV in your children's room*
  If you're planning to get a TV for your son or daughter, please think again. It's another distraction and will definitely interrupt their sleep pattern. You know that the TV will be on most of the time even if they don't really watch it.

- *Family time activities*
  Facilitate a "family time" activity at least once a week. These types of activities are rare, but should be resurrected. In the past families used to play board games like Monopoly or Scrabble. The interest seems to have died down, and these games aren't as popular anymore. Perhaps you can find something else that would be interesting for your children that would keep them occupied, or maybe it's time to go back to those good old days prior to so many technological distractions and reconsider some of those games and start playing them again. You never know, your children may enjoy it.

- *Reading time should be mandatory*
  Reading time should be required, at least one hour a day two-three times a week. Many children, including those who are doing well at school, don't like reading—they consider it boring. "I already do enough reading at school," is their number one excuse. It's not enough, especially living in this tech era where everything seems to be abbreviated, which may impact their spelling. How many times a day do they text? How many abbreviations do they have to use to make it fast and easy for themselves? Plenty. These are some of them: **U**-you, **B/C**-because, **CU**-see you, **NOYB**-none of your business, **J/K**-just kidding, **2nte**-tonight and many others. There is nothing wrong with abbreviating words if you want to send a quick message, but most children already struggle with spelling, and abbreviating words certainly won't help, but may affect their ability to spell words correctly. That is why reading is so important. Let them pick a book or a magazine of their interest as long as they read. The more they read, the more they see standard usage of words and sentences. The more reading they do, the more new words they learn.

- *Do as you say*
  Remember, as parents you are their primary teachers, you are their role models, so stick with what you say. How can children take rules seriously if you're always plugged into your gadgets? If the rule is "No cell phones at the dinner table," then you should also leave your cell phone in another room, or power it off and enjoy a nice family dinner without being interrupted by text messaging or talking to somebody while eating.

- *Don't introduce technology too soon*
  So many times I see parents giving their phones to toddlers to play while they're waiting in line at the supermarket or waiting for an appointment at the doctor's office. They do this to prevent an outburst or tantrum, as little kids don't like to wait and get tired very quickly. However, if you think about a meltdown, then think long-term how big their meltdown is going to be if they get addicted to electronic devices from such an early age. If you are taking your little ones to places that require waiting, then take something with you like their favorite toy or a book. Three- and four-year-olds don't have such a big need for special apps and screen games. The later you introduce them to all this stuff, the more enjoyable their childhood is going to be, because you are allowing them to enjoy other things in the world. Remember, one thing is to let kids maneuver a digital device, another—to encourage positive habits; teach the importance of not being addicted—put away their device when asked or when their allotted screen time is over.

Cellular Phone Addiction

Scientifically, cellular phone addiction is known as *nomophobia*, the fear of being without a cell phone. It's always with your child, and they always have access to it, almost 24/7 except school hours. This addiction can be even more serious than being hooked on computer games. Most teens want the latest and greatest smartphone (iPhones, Androids), which are more or less minicomputers that allow you to download the same apps.

Cellular phone addiction can be very serious, because it allows your children to mimic their computer and, as an added bonus, text unstoppably and, of course, make phone calls. Those children who are constantly plugged into their cell phones are very susceptible to cyber bullying, considering that predators know that children are always attached to their device. Set rules for usage and safety. Smartphones have multiple uses: downloading apps, music files, social networking—the selection is huge, but so is the probability of addiction. And unfortunately, cell phones are more difficult to monitor because you're not always with your teenager, but a cell phone is.

Children can't wait to get their hands on the latest and greatest iPhone. You know how impatient they are and how persuasive they can be, but make them agree on a set of rules like the ones I mentioned earlier before making that purchase, i.e., putting away a phone during meal times, silencing or turning off before going to bed, or other rules that you consider important.

Below are a few tips to consider before and after making that purchase of the latest smartphone:

- Be more proactive; when shopping for a cell phone, determine security features available.
- Talk to your children about the importance of not revealing cell phone numbers or passwords online.
- Remind your children that anything sent from their cell phone can be easily forwarded and shared.
- When you receive a bill, review cell phone records for any unknown numbers or night phone calls and texts.
- Some of the apps are not free, and in order to purchase them, you need to use your account or credit card; therefore, before making any purchase, review and approve the apps that your child wants to download.

By constantly reinforcing responsible use of cell phones to your children, you improve their chances to effectively manage usage and remain addiction-free.

Social Media Addiction

Social networking can be a fun activity, but it also can turn into an addiction. How many people do you know who can spend hours socializing with people on Facebook, for example? Many of them are teens. Teens gravitate to such social apps as Facebook, YouTube, Instagram, Snapchat, Twitter, and others. A typical day usually starts with checking email, text messages, and updates to their social media outlets. It doesn't stop at home: it continues in the car, bus, subway, bathroom, coffee shops, anywhere and everywhere. It seems like their whole life revolves around networking online with their friends. Some teens are more connected than others; for them communicating in a virtual world is better than in person. Even while doing homework, children still feel tempted to switch to their favorite site for a chat by typing a short line and then going back to their homework. Many adults do the same when they're at work and have a computer in front of them. It's pretty hard to break this addiction, as it requires some discipline and self-control, which most people do not have.

You can't prevent your children from social networking; for many it's their outlet, especially after a hard day of school, homework, and chores. If they still have time left over—let them have fun by socializing online with their friends if they choose, but make sure it doesn't affect your child in a negative way.

When do you have to worry:

- When your child is not very social and has trouble connecting face to face. I don't mean being shy or quiet, which may be a part of your child's personality. What I mean is when you notice your child being withdrawn, having trouble getting along with people, and becoming antisocial. You will notice it because usually it doesn't happen suddenly. It also can be a symptom of depression.

- When you see your child spending a few hours a day logged into social media sites instead of being outside and participating in physical activities. You know that fresh air is beneficial for everyone. Your children spend half of their day at school studying; then they come home and stay inside the four walls again. Not only does it affect their health, but also their mind. Children who spend time outside every day get their daily dosage of vitamin D, which contributes in bone strength and a stronger immune system. Another benefit is that time outside soothes children and lowers risks of obesity, hyperactivity, and depression. It also makes their mind sharper. Consider making time for fresh air mandatory.
- When your child has difficulty waking up for school because he or she was spending too much time socializing online the previous night instead of sleeping. It's important to set a lights-out time—it should be the same time every day with an exception for Friday and Saturday if your child wants to stay up longer and watch a movie.
- When your child uses the Internet secretly, asks for privacy while using it, and gets really upset when you enter his or her room or stand near his or her electronic device. Wanting privacy and staying in the room alone is not a bad thing, especially when children get older, but as a parent you know your child, and you can always sense that something is wrong when a child wants to keep the door closed all the time or lowers his voice, knowing that you are passing by his room, or suddenly closes the screen window on the computer. Noticing these patterns frequently can be a sign that something is wrong.
- Sometimes the addiction toward social networking and games can be so strong that you may want to seek professional help to make sure your child gets the appropriate care available.

You probably heard about *M2 Generation*—today's highly technical children whose lives revolve around the media, including television, computers, music, mobile devices, and video games. In her article "Are Kids Spending Too Much Time Online?" Katie Roof states that children spend an average of over seven hours per day online, which can cause sleep interruption, obesity, and behavioral problems. No screen viewing should be allowed any closer to one hour before bedtime. What's also important to know is that the social media service has a minimum age requirement of 13, based on the Children's Online Privacy Protection Act (COPPA). A lot of sites are starting to think about creating safer environments for children. Brands like YouTube, Twitter, and Snapchat have released children's versions of their sites to help facilitate safer searching.

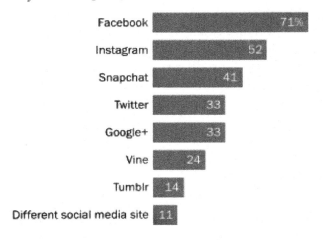

Facebook, Instagram and Snapchat Top Social Media Platforms for Teens

% of all teens 13 to 17 who use ...

Facebook	71%
Instagram	52
Snapchat	41
Twitter	33
Google+	33
Vine	24
Tumblr	14
Different social media site	11

Source: Pew Research Center's Teens Relationships Survey, Sept. 25-Oct. 9, 2014 and Feb. 10-Mar. 16, 2015. (n=1,060 teens ages 13 to 17).

PEW RESEARCH CENTER

Common Media Questions and Answers

What can I do about all the ads my children see online?

There's not much you can do without restricting your children's online time. Companies are constantly on the lookout for new and creative ways to reach kids—and they've increased ads in games and websites.

Below are a few things you can teach your kids:

- Avoid blatantly branded websites: HappyMeal, Lego, LuckyCharms, HotWheels, among many others.
- Stick to noncommercial sites or ones that reinforce your values. Usually, a child's school gives a list of websites based on a subject. The main point here is to avoid those that display constant advertisements.
- Give children an allowance. Whether it's real money, an online account, or a gift card, children who have to use their own money to pay for a downloadable app will really consider its value. A lot of computer games are purchased online today. Parents typically need to use a credit card. If I don't want to buy a game because I don't consider it necessary, but my son really wants it, then I just tell him to use money from his savings. He gives me money from his savings/piggy bank, and only then will I use my card to purchase the game. Using this method, he doesn't ask me too often.

What's the best way to talk to children about advertising?

Take advertising seriously for the sake of your children. Teaching the dos and don'ts of advertising reduces the risk posed to your children. The best way to talk to them about advertising is to indicate different ways marketers try to get their brands noticed.

Here are some ideas:

- Tell your children never to click on an ad or fill out a form without your permission. Contests and promotions are ways for companies to collect emails and phone numbers. Talk with your children about the real purpose behind promotions, downloads, and links from games and apps.
- Explain tricks advertisers use in commercials; for example, advertisers often use Vaseline to make hamburgers look juicy, animated stars to imply that a candy tastes out of this world. . . children need to know those gimmicks.
- Talk about emotional manipulation. Ask your children how they felt before and after watching an ad. Reveal how ads make people want things they don't need.
- Remind children that their self-worth is not determined by what they own, but by their character, kindness, empathy—not material stuff.

How should I deal with movies that glorify drinking or drug use?

Studies show that teens who watch movies with alcohol are more likely to binge-drink. Unfortunately, it might be challenging to find alternative entertainment without booze. Alcohol ads featuring music, animals, funny characters, humor, and a cool-looking lifestyle naturally pique children's interest, and they are more likely to have positive views about drinking alcohol. Videos of celebrities getting high contribute to a growing acceptance of weed. Ask your children who they believe more: people who entertain for a living, or doctors, scientists, and childhood-development experts who study—and warn against—the drug's ill effects.

The legality of marijuana advertising is still being worked out in the states where pot is legal, but anti-drug advocates warn that pot marketing soon will flood the airwaves. Parents will probably have a tougher time battling the influence of pot marketing as marijuana use becomes more acceptable.

Below are a few tips on how to discuss alcohol and marijuana marketing techniques with your children:

- *Impart your values*
  Most teens still listen to their parents, despite much evidence to the contrary. You still have time to discuss what's important with your children: good character, solid judgment, being responsible for your actions, and belief in a bright future—all of which could be compromised by pot and alcohol use.

- *Explain the health consequences*
  Study after study indicates that pot negatively affects a teen's developing brain and that drinking has plenty of health risks.

- *Look for warning signs*
  Studies show that drinking and smoking pot are often associated with other issues—social exclusion, school problems, and emotional instability.

- *Pull back the curtain on alcohol and pot marketing*
  Instead of lecturing, help your children dissect the ads and show them how they influence emotions, choices, and behavior.

Who is collecting my children's data, and what are they doing with it?

Companies like McDonald's can collect data every time a user visits a website. That includes anything you click on and any information you input when you fill out a form. Companies aggregate data to build composite profiles of people's habits, preferences, and purchases, which is valuable information for marketers. Next time you or your child wants to register for a free site, remember the price you pay for admission is surrendering your personal information.

What's the impact of media violence on children?

Research shows that viewing or playing violent content increases the chances that a child will engage in violent behavior later in life—especially if other risk factors are present, such as growing up in a violent home. You won't be able to avoid all exposure to violent content. The entertainment industry is always going to try to capture audiences with extreme imagery, but in your home you have control over what your children watch and play—and research shows that children whose parents actively manage their content make quality choices on their own. There may be a time when your children are ready to handle more violent media—introduce it age-appropriately and discuss it as a family.

How do I talk to my children about violence on TV, in movies, or in games?

Violence is everywhere: in video games, movies, books, music videos, and cartoons. Children are being exposed at younger ages. Talking about media violence helps to manage its impact on them.

Here are some tips for those conversations:

- Help your children tap into feelings of empathy. The more media violence children are exposed to, the more "normal" it appears. Repeated viewings can desensitize your children to others' pain and suffering. Ask them how they would feel in real life if someone they knew was badly hurt.
- Remind them that real violence isn't a joke. A lot of violence is played for laughs. But when people get hurt, that's not entertainment. You can discuss how certain situations inspire conflicting emotional reactions.
- Explain consequences. Discuss the true consequences of violence, and point out how unrealistic it is for people to get away with violent behavior.

- Teach positive conflict resolutions. Explain your values regarding violent behavior and the importance of handling disagreements nonviolently.

Be clear with your children that you want them to grow up knowing how to stand up for themselves and for what they believe, but not in a physical way. Physical violence always makes a conflict worse. You want your children to stand up for themselves in a peaceful way. Sometimes it's about being firm and assertive, sometimes just stepping away from the conflict and not escalating it.

When children are going through puberty, their behavior is changing too, and quite often it becomes more aggressive. It's typical of many teens to blame others, answer back, slam doors, swear, scream. You need to make kids understand that these behaviors are not acceptable. Create boundaries that they shouldn't cross, especially when it comes to dealing with adults. As parents, you need to know how to control your behavior too, especially when your children "push your buttons." Try to stay as calm as possible because they are watching how you handle your anger and frustration.

Here are a few tips you can teach children:

- No matter how difficult the situation is, calm down first instead of reacting right away, because it only triggers a confrontation.
- Create options and possible solutions for different situations that typically occur to children.
- Teach them how to think about win-win situations. Many people think that in order to resolve a conflict, somebody has to lose and somebody has to win. It's always good to know how to listen to each other and negotiate so everybody is a winner.
- Make them understand that not all conflicts can be avoided, and sometimes they shouldn't be, because there are certain situations in life that have to be confronted. However, with proper conflict resolution techniques they can be solved.

Should I be concerned if my tween (10-12 years old) is still frightened by violence in movies?

Although some children in this age group might start seeking out scary content, there's nothing wrong with others who dislike it. The ability to handle violence comes in time and shouldn't be forced.

How much sexual content in media is appropriate for children?

Children are exposed to sexual imagery in advertisement, on TV, in movies, in video games, and on the Internet. The more prevalent sexual situations are, the more normal they seem. Sexual images educate a child's view of sex long before they've experienced it.

Tips for parents of *elementary school-age* children:

- Sexual content should be prohibited at this age. Make sure it's blocked from their list of apps. Young children imitate what they see and repeat what they hear, even if they don't understand it.
- Use safe-search filters on search engines. Children look for images on Google and Yahoo, and even the most benign search terms can surface something inappropriate for viewing.

Tips for parents of *middle school-age* children:

- Be aware and share your values. By middle school, most children know the facts. Make sure you explain your values and balance the sexual examples children see everywhere with your family's values.
- Don't let children use TVs and computers behind closed doors.
- Look for teachable moments. A TV show in which a teen considers having sex with her boyfriend can be the perfect opening for you to talk. Ask your children what they think about.

Tips for parents of *high school-age* children:

- Discuss the differences between scripted sex and reality. At this age, your children are moving into the sexually active zone. Discuss consequences and risky behaviors.
- Indicate and educate them about safe sex.

Does watching professional sports, such as football or baseball, contribute to body image?

Children absorb more messages about body image from what you say and do more than anything else. This is a great opportunity to stress a positive body image and reinforce your values.

Here are some things to point out:

- Emphasize the idea that athletes work hard to achieve their goals—it's not about what they look like, but how they perform on the field.
- Discuss how the announcers talk about the players. Do they stress the positives: the workouts, the team atmosphere, the discipline?

Is it OK for my child to start his or her own YouTube channel?

It's not illegal for children under 13 to create social media profiles on sites that collect user data so long as the parent has approved it and is aware of the account and knows that the user's data is being collected. Create a shared account: create a log-in together (or use your Gmail address and add your child's account in the settings). With a shared account, you can review all the steps as a team. Consider keeping the password so you can log in whenever you want. You can look up for more questions and answers by logging in www.commonsensemedia.org

Cyberbullying

Cyberbullying is harassment that takes place using electronic technology: cell phones, tablets, computers, as well as communication tools including social media sites, text messages, chat, and websites. Examples of cyberbullying include nasty text messages or emails, rumors sent by email or posted on social networking sites, and embarrassing pictures, videos, websites, or fake profiles. To understand more, visit the website www. stopbullying.gov.

Quite often children who are victims of cyberbullying are those who stand out among the majority. These are children who are very shy, considered weak, and unable to defend themselves, or children who are obese, or have special needs, or quite the opposite, children who are smart and study diligently, but don't get along with their peers and have low self-esteem.

Cyberbullying can happen any time during the day or night: certain messages and images can be posted and reach a child any time. These messages and images can be posted anonymously and distributed quickly to a very wide audience. Unfortunately, it can be difficult and sometimes impossible to trace the source, just as it's difficult to delete inappropriate and harassing messages.

It's not always easy to spot cyberbullying immediately. Children are reluctant to speak with their parents about being bullied or humiliated, because they don't want to be accepted as complainers and may feel ashamed of the social stigma. Some are worried that their computer privileges will be taken away. Unfortunately, bullying can be very dangerous for your loved ones. It can cause severe depression and for children to be withdrawn, which can result in tragic outcomes such as stress-related disorders and even suicide. That is why communication and trust are so important in the family.

Here are some signs to look for with your child:

- Gets upset every time they use the Internet or a cell phone
- Is unwilling to attend school and sometimes skips it
- Receives poor grades
- Has lower self-esteem

- Seems withdrawn and moody
- Starts using alcohol and drugs

Is Your Child Being Cyberbullied

What do you do once you find out that your child has been cyberbullied?

Below are a few suggestions:

- Don't respond and don't forward cyberbullying messages, as it only makes the situation worse. However, save and even print all the threatening messages, emails, pictures for evidence.
- Block the person who is bullying.
- Report cyberbullying to your child's school: teacher, principal, counselor, superintendent or State Department of Education.
- Learn the ways to keep your children safe online. Read more about safety tips in the section titled Online Safety and How to be Proactive.

A Few Words About Sexting

Sexting or "sex texting" is sharing sexually explicit photos, videos, messages via a cell phone or the Internet (nude photos or selfies, sex acts, messages that propose or refer to sex acts). Many teens sextext because they think it's cool, they see celebrities being naked in the magazines and they want to identify with them, many girls feel pressured by their boyfriends, or it can be just peer pressure.

Many teens don't realize that all these inappropriate pictures sent via the Internet or cell phone are not really private. It takes only seconds for those pictures and images to be seen by many other users of the Internet. Besides, it can also have some serious consequences such as embarrassment and humiliation, legal consequences, and it can serve as a hindrance when it comes to college or even looking for a job, because many colleges and employers check online profiles.

Some states have adopted laws with penalties for those who send photos either by teenagers or adults. These laws are less severe for teens than adults who send sexually explicit stuff to underaged people.

Sexting laws are a relatively new phenomenon in society. Since 2009, about 19 states have adopted teen sexting laws. Though teen sexting laws are not present in a majority of states, the trend appears to be toward more widespread adoption of these laws. In the meantime, in those states without sexting laws, it may still be punishable under pre-existing laws that target child pornography (http://www.criminaldefenselawyer. com/crime-penalties/juvenile/sexting.htm).

It's important to educate children on how to remain vigilant of sex offenders who prey on children online. According to Youth Internet Safety Survey (YISS), Internet offenders manipulate young people into criminal sexual relationships by appealing to a teen's desire to be appreciated, understood, and find out more about sex. Another risky thing that young people do is looking for romantic relationships online. Young kids and teenagers are the primary victims of online offenders because of their vulnerability. Research also suggests that one quarter of the victims are boys with sexual orientation issues who get into trouble looking online for help and understanding that they normally can't get at home or school.

The only way to prevent sexting and future embarrassment is talking to your children about the consequences of sending inappropriate sexual material over the Internet. They need to understand how quickly it can get into a virtual world and stay there for a very long time, becoming an obstacle for better opportunities in the future. Your children also need to understand why it's considered a crime and why they're responsible for their actions.

Being a Tech-Safe Generation

Keeping children safe in a digital world is one of the main concerns for today's parents. Children, especially teens, need their privacy and some freedom, but they still need supervision when it comes to digital devices and media. The Internet is the most popular and available resource for many reasons: studying, chatting, playing, watching videos, and shopping. However, we need to be aware of the dangers that the Internet possesses.

According to a *Norton Online Family Report*, nearly 62% of children worldwide have had a negative experience online—nearly four in ten involving serious situations, i.e., cyberbullying or receiving inappropriate photos from strangers; 74% of children who are active on social networks say they've found themselves in unpleasant situations alone, while additional surveys reveal that nearly eight in ten have witnessed acts of meanness or cruelty on Facebook, Google+, and similar sites.

Most of the time when we hear about tech devices, we think about boys. Right? Now look at the results of the survey conducted for Common Sense Media by Knowledge Networks. The survey was completed in 2012 among teens, ages 13-17:

Girls	**Boys**
77% text daily	60% text daily
33% ever tweeted	22% ever tweeted
75% love posting photos	42% love posting photos

The danger is always there, and in order to prevent harm to their children, parents need to educate themselves first and then communicate those risks with their children. It would also be helpful if schools could contribute in preventing the overuse of technology at home and help students redirect their attention on other age-appropriate activities. It would be very helpful for both students and their parents to attend workshops at school that would emphasize the dangers of recreational technology at least to build awareness and the necessary steps that need to be taken. In his book *Wired Child*, Richard Freed states that schools should talk with their students about the risks of being a peer-follower on matters of technology. They should help kids and their parents understand that the tech-focused lifestyle normalized by our culture is a poor fit with the increasingly rigorous admission requirements for colleges. Schools can also outline what a successful student's after-school schedule typically looks like: focused study, sports, arts, or community activities rather than multitasking between fun-based technologies.

Scott Steinberg, a high-tech parenting expert, suggests the following:

- Find out what social networks your children are using and have a firm understanding of how they work. Let your children know that anything they do with technology can be tracked and monitored back to them. Many experts recommend enforcing a transparent password policy with your children, meaning every password for any login is available for parents. Set rules that if you discover any inappropriate activities have taken place, these can be grounds for immediate restriction or loss of privileges.

- No one knows exactly what the future holds; chances are your children will be applying to colleges after high school and, soon after, entering the work force. So remind them that the things they post now can and likely will be used against them, even if it's five or ten years down the line. Don't share any photos or other information that can be embarrassing or controversial to anyone.

- Talk to children about not spreading rumors, name-calling, and negative gossip online. If you can't back up what it is you are posting by being willing to say it directly to others in real life, then don't put it out there.

- Discuss the appropriate times to use technology, as well as times that should be device-free; for example they should never try to use any device that will distract them from driving.

- Educate children of online dangers and encourage them to speak up when questionable content or situations are encountered.

Teach them that the rules of communicating and playing online are pretty much the same as in real life: don't respond to strangers, don't discuss your personal problems, don't talk about your family members.

You may consider getting one of those apps that would allow you to keep track of what your children are doing. Many children are obsessed with Internet use and can be exposed to adult content that's not appropriate. There are different software applications that keep your children safe when they are online. One of the most popular is *Qustodio*, a universal app that allows parents to monitor who their children chat with by logging into social networks like Facebook, blocks harmful content from search results, and lets parents get emergency alerts when a child is in trouble. You can also check a few other services that provide online security like *Uknowkids*, *AVG Family Safety and MamaBear*.

Consider using tracking software for older teenagers, as it enables you to see which sites they've visited. This tool gives children more freedom to explore the Internet, but it also allows you to verify that they're using the Internet safely and responsibly. Let your children know that you trust them, but you still need to check which systems they're accessing when they go online. Be aware that even if you use content blockers and trackers, many teens figure out ways to get around them, so stay alert.

According to FBI Special Agent Peter A. Gulotta, Jr., "We tell our children never to talk to strangers in person, but we don't do a good job of telling them not to speak with strangers on the Internet. . . The Internet can be a valuable educational tool, and the FBI doesn't try to discourage its use. We do, however, want parents and teachers to be aware of the risks and take steps to minimize them."

Those measures should include the following:

- Establish a good relationship with children. Children who are the most vulnerable to online predators are those who are already troubled and don't have a good relationship with a trusted adult.
- Control their online environment. Don't allow children to use a screen profile or provide personal information online. Predators, Gulotta said, will put

a kid on a buddy list, look for the child whenever he or she is online, gradually become a confidante, and eventually start talking about sexual topics.

- Be frank about what's out there. There are a lot of people with terrible intentions. Children need to know that.
- Do not post a child's photo on the Internet. It's tantamount to putting personal information online. "I'm not saying your child is going to be hurt if his picture is on the Internet. I'm saying they could be. Know what the parameters are; know what these people are doing; and then make your own decisions."

According to Gulotta, middle school students and other young teens are most vulnerable to online dangers, because they have greater access to the Internet than younger students, are often less closely supervised, and are more willing to participate in discussions about emotions and relationships.

If a child reports being approached online, immediately write down as much information as possible, including the screen name or email address of the person who contacted the child. For additional information on child safety, visit the site www.educationworld.com.

The following are resources you can use to teach your children how to be tech safe:

- The Modern Parent's Guide High-Tech Parenting Tips
- Common Sense Media
- Norton Family Safety Guide
- Enough is Enough Internet Safety 101 Quiz
- NetSmartz and Common Sense Media Workshops are interactive sites that will provide you with a lot of information on safety that you can review together with your children. Common Sense Media is a nonprofit organization that promotes education and advocacy for families. It also reviews movies, video games, apps, and websites and rates them in terms of age-appropriate content. This site has a lot of good information for cyber world users.

NetSmartz Workshop is an educational program from the National Center for Missing and Exploited Children (NCMEC) that provides age-appropriate resources to help children be safe on and offline. This program is designed for children, parents, and educators. By the way, if you are planning to set the rules for your children regarding Internet use or maybe you want to put them in writing and create a contract, NetSmartz is a good site to check, because it has different pledges for children regarding Internet use, and it categorizes them according to the child's age: Primary, Intermediate, Middle and High School. Here is an example of a Safety Pledge regarding Internet Safety Rules that fall into a category of Primary:

- I will tell my trusted adult if anything makes me feel sad, scared, or confused.
- I will ask my trusted adult before sharing information like my name, address, and phone number.
- I won't meet face to face with anyone from the Internet.
- I will always use good netiquette and not be rude or mean online.

There are many other tips, advice, and tutorials that are worth checking by clicking www.netsmartz.org

What is Digital Citizenship

Digital Citizenship is a concept pioneered by organizations like the Family Online Safety Institute (FOSI), in which parents, schools, and other technology leaders and institutions recommend focusing energy on preparing children for a tech-centric society by teaching them about appropriate methods to use technology, as opposed to focusing on the potential negative outcomes of technology.

The reality is that many of the social customs that apply to real-life interactions are best applied online. If you saw another child being bullied or beat up, you'd tell a grownup about it, so do the same if you are online. The roots of digital citizenship are positive real-life interactions and activities that can and should be translated to the virtual world (Scott Steinberg, "Technology and Kids: A High-Tech And Online Parenting Guide").

Think about digital citizenship as a way to learn about digital ethics, which is very similar to real life situations. If you want to learn more about this concept, go to www.digitalcitizenship.net.

Reflection Questions

After digesting everything above ask yourself:

- How much screen time a day/week is enough for my children?
- Do I know which social network sites my children use?
- How can I track what my children are posting or who they're chatting online with?
- How do I protect my children's privacy online?
- Do my children see me as a trusted parent, just in case they get into trouble or something goes wrong, they'll feel comfortable to talk?
- What computer/media skills do my children need that can be vital for their future?

If you want to establish a good foundation for your children's development, then you have to add some structure in their life by setting rules and sticking to them. Educate your children about safety, create family time, and always communicate with them. Be aware that lack of communication at home makes them look for comfort in front of the screen as a way to escape painful feelings and situations, which could eventually turn your child into a loner.

Compare the time your children spend on media versus other activities, and show them how to achieve the right balance by teaching them how to adhere to their priorities first. This is the most effective way to embrace technology.

Preparing Your Children for Adulthood

It all starts at home. Not only are you responsible for raising your children, but also for their success, or let's say for teaching them the habits that would contribute to their success. To improve their odds, start imposing behaviors early in their childhood. Besides teaching your children good habits (i.e., manners, respect, etc.), teach them how to be structured.

The earlier you start, the smoother the transition. Children who are raised with structure are more responsible and productive later on in life. You may have a few disagreements and probably rebellious situations (or maybe not), but your children will have a sense of responsibility to focus on their priorities first.

I've been talking about technology in the life of our children and how destructive and helpful it can be at the same time. Honestly, it's really up to us parents to help our children use technology to their advantage. If children are not managed properly, it could severely affect the quality of their life now and in the future.

As we discuss our children in the digital generation, it's very important to draw a line between educational and recreational media consumption. You want to raise tech-smart, not tech-obsessed children. To achieve this, you have to first look at your family routines, modifying the ones that are not working too well and establishing some new ones. It all starts with us parents, who are the most important teachers in a child's life. After all, you are the ones who mentored them before they saw their first teacher. They emulated you before they even started school. When children are little, they emulate their parents' behavior, words, and actions. This is the best time to start "family rules" or "policies" that will contribute to your children's well-being, which includes academic, emotional, financial, and social success. Your children spend half of their day in school, where they learn academics, cognitive skills, how to socialize with other children, how to listen, follow directions, and be respectful towards their teachers. However, in order to institute those skills and good habits, they need to be reinforced at home. Just studying and going to school are not enough. Besides, don't forget that at school the teacher has many students in the classroom and limited time, which makes it impossible to give each student the same quality time and attention as you can give your child as parents.

Moreover, teachers today are obligated to prepare students for state exams by cutting down on a lot of creative and interesting topics (i.e., art, music, and gym activities are significantly reduced). It's something for parents to consider and figure out how to bring creative things back into their children's life.

As a teacher, I see a big difference between children whose parents just attend to basic needs (feeding, dressing, bathing, transportation) and children whose parents go beyond those basic requirements. When parents spend quality time with their children by communicating frequently, reading to them, doing interesting things together like art projects, cooking and playing brain-stimulated games, children tend to be well-rounded, usually excited about learning, have good self-help skills, and are even more confident than those who don't receive "quality family time." And because we live in a digital age, media use and consumption also play an important role in raising a competent and confident child.

In the book *The Learning Habit* (I recommend this book to every parent and educator), the authors state that the best thing you can do for your children is to prepare them for a successful future by providing enduring learning habits, because the ability to learn is what will help them succeed in life. "There is a growing gap between the life a child has in their parent's home and the life they can expect as adults." They believe there are two methods that contribute to developing strong habits: *empowerment parenting* that begins with how we interact with our children on a daily basis, and *creating opportunities* for our children to develop the eight essential learning habits:

- Media management
- Academic homework and reading
- Time management
- Goal-setting
- Effective communication
- Responsible decision-making
- Concentrated focus
- Self-reliance

These skills are the backbone of a successful life. They can be developed through habits, and habits can be built through rules that require accountability and consistency. Besides, children need to learn how to make choices and be responsible for their consequences. For example, you made it a rule for your children to pack their school bag every evening, making sure they pack everything for the next day. Initially you will remind them to pack their bag and get ready for the next day, but after a short period of time your children will get used to packing it on their own without being reminded. However, if for some reason your son forgets to put in something important like a homework assignment, don't go to school to bring it to him—he needs to experience the consequences of forgetting important stuff and to be more vigilant next time, which will never happen if he relies on you as their savior. He needs to hold himself accountable to be successful.

Are Your Children Prepared for the Future

I came across the article "Smart but Helpless Kids" by Kim Abraham and Marney Studaker that talks about our children's future and how well we prepare them. The article emphasizes our digital generation and the skills our children are learning. They are tech savvy, but they are not really prepared to be survivors and live a successful life on their own. Why? Because parents do everything for them. "Over the past several decades, our society has moved increasingly more towards 'doing for' our children rather than 'teaching how.' Are there things that you are doing for your child that he is capable of doing for himself? What about those other skills? The ones that get us through emergencies, budget crunches, stressful situations, and daily tasks that require perseverance and problem solving? How can we strengthen this generation's life skills?"

Years ago, children were busy helping parents with housework and raising younger siblings, as well as doing work outside the house, so they were raised as young adults who would be prepared for life's challenges by having acquired those necessary life skills. In the 'Old Days,' children played an essential role in the survival of the family. They helped farm the land, feed the livestock, gathered eggs and prepared meals. Over time, a child's role became less of a contributor and more of a receiver. Instead of earning material things for helping the family survive, today expensive items (i.e., computers, televisions, phones) became Christmas and birthday gifts.

I suggest that parents have a look at how much their children can do and could do if they were properly mentored. There are simple things that our children can learn while they are still living at home and also afterwards apply these skills in their own life. It can be as simple as having children make their own bed in the morning, clean the bathroom, babysit a younger sibling, help in the kitchen by chopping vegetables for a salad, making a sandwich, and washing dishes. Determine what would be reasonable for your child's age. They don't have to be one-sided: good with tech devices and studying, they can be ahead of the game if you train them by taking little steps that are within their ability. This is what it means to be a good parent: you may not be tech savvy like your child, but you can teach them many other things and skills that they wouldn't be able to survive without and be well adept to life. I simply call them "life skills." And one day your children will be very thankful for these skills.

Be careful not to underestimate your child's abilities. Are there things you're doing for them that they are capable of doing for themselves? If so, the next time your child needs to return some jeans at the mall, instead of taking them up to the sales clerk yourself, consider coaching them through it, from walking up to the counter to showing the receipt to actually making sure they get the correct amount of money back. I think there is a lesson for all of us here. We tend to do too much for our children because we are afraid to distract them from what they are doing even if what they are doing is not so important. Sometimes it's even faster for us to do some stuff by ourselves like making their bed or cleaning up the bathroom than asking our children to do it. We need to start thinking about their life and future not only in terms of college, but also in terms of living on their own, taking care of themselves and being more confident due to multiple skills they now possess.

Expanding a Child's Mind Beyond School

When we think about education, the first things that come to our minds are usually school, teachers, books, homework. However, there are many other factors that contribute to a child's education. Education goes far beyond these nomenclatures as children need to develop life skills. They can learn things from reading, seeing, and hearing outside of school that interest them and expand their knowledgebase.

I believe education always starts and continues at home. This is the place where children are influenced the most on their attitude towards things, people, and their overall outlook on life. And, of course, parents are the most important people in every child's life because they are considered their primary teachers. They are the ones who can help extend their child's knowledge beyond school and acquire the skills that are necessary to succeed in life.

Why isn't going to school enough? At school children learn academic skills, but they may not know how to apply those skills successfully in life. They may be good students and get good grades, but they have very little knowledge on how to maneuver and develop key skills for the real world. Many of these children need their parents' influence when it comes to life because they know their children's strengths, weaknesses, and insecurities. I am not saying that all children should choose their career path based on parental guidance; many know what they want to do without their parents' involvement.

The goal of all parents should be contributing to their children's education in all facets of life. Don't neglect the full potential of their minds just by sending them to school and having teachers do their job. This is not enough. How many children, even those who do well at school, are empty inside? Plenty. Just like there are plenty of adults who are empty inside because they don't put any effort into developing nonacademic skills.

There are ways to expand your child's mind by including some extra activities. They can be as simple as reading, watching the Discovery Channel, listening to the news, learning how to play chess, going to the museum and the theatre, seeing shows or musicals, learning to play a musical instrument, and reading the newspaper. There are many ways you can increase your child's interests or develop new ones.

Reading is really important, even though many children and adults overlook it because they don't like it. Find something your children are interested in: if it's not books, then it could be magazines and articles related to their interests or hobbies. When children get older, you may want to introduce them to reading newspapers or viewing the news online so they learn how to keep themselves updated with current events. A good way to make them interested in reading news is to set an example. When children see their parents read magazines and newspapers and discuss what they've read, they will be more willing to pick up that habit, too. In the beginning, you can choose an article or two for your kids to read, knowing that it contains something that will interest them, and then discuss the content, ask for their opinion, ask what they would do, and how they would act. Enable them to express themselves by learning how to agree and disagree, because this promotes further thinking and a desire to engage. By doing this, they're expanding their mind. Your children don't just discuss pertinent topics; they learn how to think, evaluate information, and look for solutions. They also learn how to articulate properly and logically. Teach them how to scan through newspapers and magazines quickly. Show them how to utilize skimming and scanning techniques. Thinking is a skill, and to excel, it needs to be practiced like any other skill. Make thinking fun for your children and engage them in discussions as often as you can by showing how much you value their opinion.

People who are good at many things usually have more choices in life than those who are good at only one thing even if they do it well. It's so important to encourage children to participate in extra activities. When they're involved in other interests, they develop new skills that make them more versatile. It provides children with confidence and helps them be more independent. There's some talent in everyone, and many children have special talents that if discovered early, can have a tremendous impact on their life. But this talent needs to be noticed. Sometimes even parents don't know that their child is talented until some extra activities kick something in and they get engaged and practice what wasn't available to them before. By participating in extra activities, children learn more about themselves, their talents, and strengths that can also contribute to making future decisions. And don't underestimate physical activities. Not only do physical activities have health benefits like boosting metabolism and improving blood circulation, but they add more mental alertness and stamina. Physical activities make children more energetic and enthusiastic.

Introduce children to museums, which open up a whole new world of imagination and exploration. Don't underestimate the importance of going to museums and their relevance in a child's education. It's a good place for them to explore and learn new things, which definitely influence their intellectual growth and development. The earlier you start taking your children to museums, the better. Lifelong learning begins at a young age, and museums are a great place to spark children's interest in art, history, and science, as well as introduce them to unknown worlds. Of course, not all children show a genuine interest in art or history; most of them need to be encouraged and helped to enjoy it, but it's absolutely doable and worth it. When children are very young, like preschool age, don't plan on staying at the museum for hours. They will get bored. However, whether you spend two hours or thirty minutes, there's always value in looking at art and interesting inventions with your children. Seeing everything can be overwhelming; therefore, create a plan to see the works of art that you consider important. Highlight things: discuss colors, texture, shapes. Make a visit to the museum educational and fun for your entire family. Many museums have exhibits for young children that offer hands-on experiences and play.

Good grades and test scores are important because they help your children go to better schools and colleges. But good grades and even good schools don't always prepare children for a successful future or the "real world," because education is more than academic success. The importance of studying well, doing homework, preparing for tests, and passing them is the number one priority, but the criteria for academic success isn't always a direct path to lifetime success. High test scores in school don't always correlate to adult accomplishments. Success builds on something more meaningful. Curiosity, thinking out of the box, creativity, the ability to communicate with people can take your children much farther than just going to school and getting good grades.

The Importance of Homework

Homework habits teach children self-mastery,
autonomy, intrinsic motivation, and self-efficacy.

From "The Learning Habit"

Good habits should begin with your children's homework. In order to do homework properly and efficiently, children need to acquire those habits that would allow them to complete it in a timely manner, leaving time for other activities: reading, doing chores, playing sports, and screen time, in other words, managing their myriad of activities effectively to promote a balanced life.

You need to start with time allocation: decide how much time your child should spend on homework based on their grade, their studying or working pace, and the amount of homework your child normally receives.

Why am I even highlighting the importance of homework? Isn't it obvious? *First*, your children learn new things at school, and it's reinforced via homework. *Second*, your children push themselves by completing challenging tasks, therefore developing cognitive skills. *Third*, your children get to experience self-sufficiency and accomplishing tasks, which make them believe in themselves. *Fourth*, your kids learn how to complete things in a quality manner. And *fifth*, if they receive a good grade for their homework, they get excited because it serves as a reward.

Don't let your children rush through their homework and don't let them stay up late before they start. Homework should be done as soon as they get home from school with their cell phones turned off. It's a fact that if you stay up late to accomplish brain-intensive activities, you are not as effective. Although you may not feel tired, your brain is. Teach your children how to plan properly so they can manage their time effectively. If they have too much homework, for example, a big project that is due in a few days, show them how to break it into small segments and do something every day so they don't have to leave everything until the last moment and then be stressed out. It's especially helpful to those children who have a very short attention span and get overwhelmed quickly. I like the idea of breaking down an assignment and working on it in small chunks—it's one of the learning habits I acquired as a child and I used as an adult. Even today, when it comes time to do my lesson planning for the next week, I never leave it for the weekend. Lesson planning takes a long time; therefore, I start doing it on Monday and do a little bit every day, so by Saturday I am done with it and I can enjoy my weekend doing what I love and spending time with my family.

Teaching Time Management

Managing time effectively is a prerequisite for success. You know the difference between how much you can accomplish during the day if you planned in advance and focused on your tasks versus doing everything spontaneously. The earlier you start teaching your children how to manage time, the easier it will be for everybody in the family, especially when it comes to completing homework or even getting ready for school in the morning.

Below are a few tips on how to teach your children good time management skills:

- Start with time estimation: have your child guess how much time it takes to perform simple functions like walking from home to school, brushing their teeth, or finishing an assignment. People in general always underestimate how long activities take. Start them at a young age to be cognizant of time.
- Use an analog clock, because it has hands that move and depicts how quickly time passes by. They can look at the clock and measure small activities in minutes (i.e., five-minute chunks).
- We all know how slow children are in the morning; everything takes twice as long. This is a huge problem for most parents, as mornings are pretty hectic and

they have to get ready for work. If you want your children to speed up with the essentials (i.e., getting dressed, making their bed, etc.), try by playing "beat the clock." Teaching children at a young age to "beat the clock" or "beat that number" is an essential tool to help them manage time to always be mindful of the most precious resource we have. Besides teaching them how to get faster, it excites them, too. You can also use a timer, especially if children take 5 to 10-minute breaks between homework assignments.

- Teach children how to prioritize daily activities: homework, chores, extra activity, and family time. Talk about the consequences of poor choices. If they play before doing their homework, they will be more tired, which will impact the quality of their homework. They will also have to go to bed late and will have a hard time waking up in the morning. Teach your children that by adhering to their top priority first (which is the dreaded unwanted homework), it makes them enjoy their free time later as they will feel relieved. The same goes with long-term projects. Let your children use an organizer or a big calendar, where they will write down their projects' due dates and then establish daily assignments to complete the project before its due date. Train them to complete their school-related project a few days before it's due. If your children have a three-day weekend or are on winter break, make them finish when their break begins so they can enjoy the rest of their time off.

Positive Reinforcement

Is it always helpful?

Praising children especially when they try to do their best at school and at home is very important and inspiring; however, you need to use praising with purpose and it has to be specific, not just "Good job" or " Way to go" or "You are the best." It's a worthless praise because it's very general and has no real value to a child. Be specific when you praise; otherwise you don't reinforce anything. Besides, some children get used to praise so much that they expect to be praised all the time; otherwise they may get upset. Praise should be realistic. You hear some parents who exaggerate praise like: "You are gorgeous," "You are awesome," "You are such a genius," or "One day you will become a famous singer." The problem is that even though children enjoy this kind of praise, subconsciously it imposes parents' expectations on children, which can cause an inner conflict later in life. The reality is that people who are awesome, gorgeous, geniuses are pretty rare in the real world. When a child gets used to this kind of over-praise, when they enter school and see that there's somebody smarter or more beautiful or more special and popular among classmates, their self-esteem may decrease, considering that in school there won't be as much praise and attention as at home.

Praise your children in moderation and make sure that praise is very realistic and specific. If a child struggles with academics, but works hard and does his best and finally makes progress, it is reflected by receiving better grades; then there's definitely room for praise. It's also important to praise children for their personal qualities and how they behave or act toward other people. Show your children that you really appreciate the fact that they are being helpful, kind, and compassionate, as it encourages them to be good human beings. Impose good values on your children that contribute to them making the right choices when it comes to interacting with people.

Teaching Healthy Competition

Your children are surrounded by competition both at home and at school even though they may not be aware of it, especially when they are still very young. However, teaching children how to develop a spirit of achievement and self-challenge is very important for their development and future opportunities. It means you have to teach your children how to compete and deal with unpleasant experiences, which will come across in their lifetime. Children need to learn how to cope with unsuccessful experiences.

Some children are born to be competitive: they always want

to be the best or the first one picked to participate in sports activities. They love to win. It's especially common for those children who are raised in families with competitive parents, who promote competition from an early age. There's nothing wrong with promoting competition at an early age as long as it's healthy competition that inspires children to try and do their best. Although not all parents and children are competitive, it's still a good idea for children to learn to compete by wanting to do their best and always try to accomplish more.

The way to teach children competition should be balanced and gradual, not stressful. Competition shouldn't be so intense that children feel pressured. It's not about losing or winning; it's about doing their best. As parents, you should encourage your children to try as many things as possible or available to them in terms of personal and academic growth. It's a good idea to start children competing against themselves, "personal best." It can be applied to school grades, sports, art projects, inventions, etc. It's important to teach a child to respect competitors and instead of getting upset in case they lose, learn from the experience and think of what can be done better next time. Praise your children for their efforts and performance rather than for winning alone. A good thing about competition is that it helps children develop healthy attitudes about winning and losing. They learn how to push themselves to the limits and get to know their abilities, especially in sports. Healthy competition builds up confidence and self-esteem. However, stay away from the competition that causes physical and emotional injury, hostility, or aggression— all this undermines your child's self-confidence. And, of course, it should never be done just for the parents' benefit.

Don't look at competition as something negative because competition can teach children self-respect and how to cope with emotions like jealousy and discontent. As a parent, you know your children's strengths, and you can support them by having your son participate in activities that are challenging and enjoyable. The only thing you should remember is not to put too much emphasis on competition, especially when children are still young: competition is not only about winning, but also about trying, evolving, maturing, learning to overcome losses, and being a team player.

Peer Pressure

It's almost impossible to avoid peer pressure. Children are surrounded by friends, classmates, siblings, or even somebody they see and admire on TV. They are dying to belong: children want to be a part of a group and feel that they belong to a community, especially if they are new or less experienced or afraid to stand out. Quite often kids do something that they would never even think of doing if it wasn't for those who they're surrounded by and put pressure on them by suggesting something they may not necessarily think of doing on their own. Children who don't want to be isolated follow a particular group; then they give in to doing things that they wouldn't normally do. Peer pressure can influence kids in terms of choosing friends, eating habits, drug and alcohol use, academic performance, and fashion choices.

Children need to be taught the right values and priorities from the time they are still very young, so they know what's important and the difference between right and wrong. Children and later teens are more aware of these priorities when they're constantly reinforced by actions and role modeling that comes from parents.

Below are some tips to teach your children on how to handle peer pressure:

- The importance of being an individual who has his or her own opinions.
- Explain the importance of saying "no" and sticking with what is right. Paying attention to their own feelings will help them make the right decisions.
- It's hard, but they need to learn how to stand up for themselves if they are picked on or made fun of by not trying certain things that peers try to impose. If they don't feel comfortable doing something, they should never do it. Inner strength and confidence help children to stay firm and walk away from trouble or danger.
- It's important to be surrounded by the right people who have similar interests and who are good

influences, rather than hanging out with the "cool" crowd just to be popular.

- Explain how essential it is to think about consequences ahead of time before it's too late. They need to ask themselves these questions before engaging in something they're not sure about: Will it hurt me physically? Will it cause me problems with law or at school? Will it hurt my parents when they find out about it?
- Show children how they can think of peer pressure as competition or "competitive" peer pressure: being stronger than "them" and not caving in to what's wrong. Explain that by doing the right things over and over, they build up a strong personality that makes them unique and serves as a big asset.

There's also good peer pressure. Your children can hang out with friends who are very competitive when it comes to sports; for example, your children may want to participate in sports and learn to be competitive or get into better shape, which would cause your child to eliminate bad eating habits and start exercising to lose weight and look good.

Morning and Evening Routines

Most successful people have discipline and live a structured lifestyle, but there are many who are very unstructured, and their life is full of clutter and inefficiencies. It's one of the main reasons they can't progress in life; they never have enough time for anything and always feel tired and sluggish. Initiating change and getting more organized is possible and never too late, although it may not be easy, especially if you were not taught how to be organized. The best way for people to be structured is to have it imposed on them when they are still children. Parents are the ones who should teach their children organizational skills and techniques that are prerequisites to success. One of the most effective ways to do it is to start with a simple morning and evening routine. These routines should be taught, executed, and constantly reinforced until they become automatic for your child.

Children need step-by-step instructions: what time should they wake up, what has to be done in the morning and in the evening, and what time they should go to sleep. Once they start performing those rituals, their life and yours will be less stressful and more efficient, considering that days are always challenging and unpredictable. Your mornings will be more streamlined, and you won't have to be stressed out, especially if you're always in a rush to get to work on time after meeting the needs of everybody in the household first.

Many parents are stressed out in the morning because their children are disorganized. It all starts with making a child get out of bed, which takes a long time, then waiting until they choose clothes to wear, then wasting time on packing homework, then you get upset, and tensions rise.

A better way to do it

The hardest task for many parents is to get their child out of bed. To make it less stressful, start waking them up 20-30 minutes ahead of time. You can try to place an alarm clock next to them, but it doesn't work with everybody; some children just ignore it and can only be awakened physically by a parent. If you wake up your child ahead of time, you will alleviate a good part of your morning stress. After washing their face and brushing their teeth, children start looking for clothes to wear, and it can be time consuming, too; that is why you should make your children lay out clothes before going to bed as a part of the evening routine. When they reach the kitchen, it's time to eat breakfast. There shouldn't be any backpacking in the morning, because it wastes time. Backpacks have to be prepared in the evening after completing their homework. You will see how much time is saved in the morning by following these simple steps. You will be in a much better mood. Your son and daughter will also eventually enjoy the efficiencies of a routine.

Below are examples of a morning and evening routine.

The Morning Routine

- Waking up 20-30 minutes before it's officially time to get up

- Washing their face and brushing their teeth. Some children, especially older ones, prefer to take a shower in the morning. Though, if a shower or a bath is taken in the evening, it saves time especially if your child needs to dry his or her hair
- Getting dressed by not spending time on picking an outfit, which is supposed to be prepared the night before
- Breakfast
- If there's some time left after finishing breakfast before leaving for school, your child can find something else to do like read a book or watch TV for a few minutes (if you don't mind) or feed a pet
- Leaving for school

The Nighttime Routine

- Preparing their backpack with their completed homework assignments, including all the letters/notes that you as a parent have to sign
- Checking a school calendar to see if there are any special events the next day or if there's a gym class so children won't forget to take their gym clothes, which should also be prepared in the evening
- Laying out clothes for the next day
- Taking a shower or a bath

Stick with these routines consistently until they become automatic for your child. It usually takes a while to make it habitual, but eventually doing these things will become a lifetime habit that will make your child's life more structured and successful, and you will enjoy the peace of mind.

Imagine a string with beads on it. The beads represent your goals, relationships, and priorities. Tip the string this way or that way, and the beads easily slide off and onto the floor. But tie a knot on each end of the string, and the beads stay put. Those knots are your morning and evening routines. They keep the priorities of your life from falling apart and thus help you progress and become a better man (Brett McKay, the author and founder of the manliest website www.ArtofManliness.com).

Spirituality

Many people get confused about spirituality; they think that being spiritual is the same as being religious. Being spiritual doesn't require you to be affiliated with a religion or denomination. It also doesn't mean you have to go to church or temple unless it is meaningful and it makes you feel good. My definition of spirituality is the ability to tap into my inner strength and find faith to push through challenging situations and difficult circumstances. Did you ever see people who've experienced hard times in their lives (the loss of a loved one or going through serious illness), and still they had a good outlook and displayed gratitude towards life? How can they do that? What's their secret? I'm sure that these are spiritually rich individuals who understand the value of life and live it by faith. It seems like nothing can break them or bring them down. They find joy in every day and are thankful to God for their existence.

Spirituality is also about having an understanding of something greater than you, the Higher Power, or what it means to many people—God. Our children need to know how to find their inner strength in order to deal with their own challenges while experiencing different milestones. For some children it's easy, but for many it's not. Most children need to be taught how to press through difficulties and find faith to execute. Faith is very closely connected to the concept of spirituality. Faith can help children guide their way through life. It can help them deal with crisis, resist peer pressure, and avoid negative influences such as drugs and alcohol.

I believe that one of the first spiritual rules that you have to teach your children is the *Golden Rule*. There are many different formulations of this rule, but the idea is the same: *Treat others the way you would like to be treated.* This rule is considered to be the ultimate rule of morality and used by many anti-bullying organizations. This rule goes beyond just being nice to people who we know or deal with on a daily basis. The Golden Rule is also about choosing the right words and doing good deeds for people who we don't know or encounter for the first time in our life. For example, when you're in line at the grocery store and a person in front of you is a few dollars short, would you be willing to offer a few dollars and help? I see so many people who are willing to help even though they don't know the person in front of them. And what's the best way to teach our children to abide by this rule—leading them by example?

One day I was switching TV channels, and I came across Joyce Meyer, a famous preacher whose sermons fulfill my spiritual needs more than anyone else. In her preaching she mentioned that if you want to mature and grow in life, then you have to follow an important principle, which isn't easy. It goes like this: *Even if it feels wrong, you still have to do what's right.* In other words, if your boss is in a bad mood and yells and it's directed at you, treat him nicely and with respect. Don't gossip behind his back and don't complain to others. If your coworker talks behind your back saying things that aren't true and hurtful, don't lash out at him and start doing the same thing behind his back. You can address the issue and talk about how you feel, but you still treat the person with respect.

The same goes for our children. If they could live by this rule, they would avoid many misunderstandings and conflicts that sometimes occur when they're in school. Let's say your son doesn't like his teacher because he says the teacher is unfair, always fault-finding and picking on him. When things like this happen, children usually lose interest in studying, become very resistant to whatever the teacher asks them to do, and even worse—they start arguing and answering back, which will eventually get them into more trouble. However, by doing what's right even when it feels wrong, your child can avoid trouble. It's important for you to approach the teacher and talk to her one-on-one after school as soon as possible, if it's possible (if not, you should set up an appointment and meet with her to clarify the situation). Your son should continue to follow the teacher's directives without being rebellious or displaying a nasty attitude. By the way, if for some reason you don't like your son's teacher, you still shouldn't criticize her in front of your son because by doing this, you're setting him up for failure. In my opinion, a teacher should always be respected—first of all, for being older than your child, and second of all, for the job that she does—educating them and being responsible for their safety while they're in the classroom.

I must admit, it's very hard for me to live by this rule, and quite often I have to clench my teeth to do what's right when I don't feel like I should. But I noticed, that when I make an effort and do what's right, later on I feel relieved and happy that I did it. It's very challenging to live by this rule, but once you master it, these actions will take your life to a different level.

How many times did you hear the phrase, *What goes around comes around* or *What you sow you will reap?* It's called the law of cause and effect, or *karma*. This spiritual law is related to Buddhism and very close to the Golden Rule. This law is also about making choices, especially when dealing with other people. Always ask yourself about the consequences of whatever choices you make. How will this choice affect you and other people? The law of karma means that for all the good actions that you perform, you get good reactions, and if you hurt somebody or display violence—you will receive the same in return one day. The law of karma states that everything that you experience today is the result of your past activities, and if you wish that your life be different in the future, you have to change your activities in the present. Some would say this is nonsense, because there are many good people who experience hardships in their life and have been mistreated by others. It's true, but we don't know how these people lived their lives in the past, and we don't know all the nuances of their lives. And even if they didn't deserve to go through hardships, it's probably a test that life presents. We all go through different life tests by constantly asking "why me?" I believe that it's important even if we are tested to keep a positive attitude and treat other people kindly and with respect no matter what we are experiencing.

Your children will also benefit from this way of thinking, especially when they get older and go through different issues with friends, classmates, peers, teachers. . . I am sure if you introduce them to the law of karma and reinforce it, they will think twice before doing something revengeful. This allows them to move forward with their lives without looking back and feel offended. For me it equals personal freedom; if only I knew about this law when I was very young, it could have saved me so much aggravation.

These are many basic principles of spirituality. Try to introduce your children to these values gradually. As I mentioned before, you don't have to be religious to be spiritual; spirituality is about knowing the basic laws of life and following them if you want to be successful and live it without regrets and guilt. It's also about teaching your children how to tap into their inner strength and see that the power to overcome challenges lies within them.

It's hard to explain to children what spirituality is, especially when they are very young. Teach them how spiritual principles can be applied in life; provide real-world examples. When kids get older, they start questioning many things, and if you communicate effectively with them then as a parent, you are the one who is going to be questioned. You may not even know all the answers, and that's OK. You can think of an answer or the best solution together. By doing this, you will contribute to your child's ability to process situations and apply solutions. Help your children deal with frustration, anger, and other reactive behaviors so they don't harm anyone.

Start with one rule at a time, explain it, talk about it, give examples, and when you apply a certain principle in your life, make a point of it to your child; explain why you decided to act in the manner you did so it will be easily understood. If you do it consistently, you will notice that your children will learn good deeds and actions and start applying them toward their friends or other adults. They will be more compassionate and more aware of their choices. Eventually, your child will be more prone to take personal responsibility during uncomfortable situations.

There are families where parents dedicate time every morning or evening to reading the Bible. This is a good habit that sets the right tone every day. Why not introduce Bible reading to your children? There are Bibles for children that are comprehensive. It's important to read it together, because you need to explain to your child the meaning of the words and verses, provide examples where applicable, and show them how it can be applied in daily life, as well as the lesson your child can draw from the content that was read. Link the ideas that are taught to their own lives so they can become more self-reflective and open-minded. And by the way, it's not just about reading; it's about studying, remembering, and putting it into practice.

Set time aside for a prayer and make the process interesting. It doesn't have to be a formal prayer; it can be a self-made prayer, as long as your child knows what he is requesting. Prayer can be helpful in life: it gives you comfort, peace, and connection to some greater force.

I am a big believer in writing down certain scriptures, or for those who don't read the Bible, some spiritual mantras that can be very comforting or inspiring, and recite them over and over again. Teach your children to do the same thing: let them have a notebook where they can write down inspirational quotes and paste pictures that mean something to them. They can even create their *vision board* with images that help them express their desires and dreams, as well as look for opportunities to achieve those dreams. They may need help in the beginning, so take time to sit down with your children and make plans for personal growth and change.

How are spiritually educated children different from those who are not? First of all, they have certain habits that are very important when it comes to experiencing life.

Below are a few habits of spiritually educated children:

- A habit of reverence: reverence towards older people, parents, teachers, God. They will think twice before answering back and arguing when it doesn't make sense.
- Compassion and hospitality toward people.
- Forgiveness.
- Responsibility for the choices they make.
- A sense of ethics and morals.
- Respect for parents and elders.

When children become more spiritual, they start listening to their true voice, or it can be called conscience or intuition, those things that protect us and keep us away from danger. Children who don't follow peer pressure and stay away from dangerous things are quite often those who listen to their inner voice. These children desist from negative behaviors more readily. These are also children who stand up for themselves in positive, but assertive ways.

More spiritual people tend to be happier than those who are not: they know how to make themselves happy, and also, they don't look for approval from anybody—they are complete and satisfied on their own. They know how to enjoy their own company because they know how to explore things on their own and keep themselves busy.

It's important to create a positive environment for children that would give them a solid emotional foundation. Try not to argue in front of them or talk negatively about other people. Don't compare your children to others, because it only creates doubt and insecurity as well as approval seeking. Create an environment that promotes success for your children.

Epilogue

Wow, what an ordeal! I knew that trying to bring Alex out of her *virtual* world and being acclimated into the *real* world would be a daunting endeavor, but the magnitude of the effort involved even caught me by surprise. After successfully mentoring several teens with cellular, social media, drug, and video game addictions, I thought I was prepared to take on Alex; boy, did I have a rude awakening.

What I learned

By far, teenage girls are the most challenging to mentor because many can be highly emotional (especially during their menstrual cycle). Also, for many, their friends are the real priority, and they overdramatize everything. Yup, it was a brutal experience. Will she have setbacks? Maybe. Will she get distracted? Without a doubt. Will she digress back to her addiction? I don't think so. She actually likes being in control of her life and productive.

Before I started mentoring her, I would shake my head in disbelief, watching the way she managed her day, or a better depiction is how she didn't. No matter how many times I told her, "Alex, spending 10-20 hours a week with your friends (via text, phone calls, social media outlets, in person, etc.) was going to prevent you from completing your goals." That got nowhere. "You need to worry about managing yourself, because in the end it's all about holding the person in the mirror accountable." Still, there was no urgency to operate like an adult, although she kept reminding me almost daily that she was one. Even with all these issues, including no common sense or self-discipline, I didn't hesitate; I decided to help her thrive as an adult.

The ordeal I endured lived up to its billing; it was brutal, but I put the onus on me for not beginning the mentoring sooner. Unfortunately many of you are in the same boat with your children. We're all busy, actually drained each evening. Knowing that her mom wasn't a very disciplined individual, it was going to be left up to me to arm her with the skills to succeed. If I could pull this off, it was going to be one of my most rewarding accomplishments.

Although I was highly successful, my biography didn't bring value to the table because I was the parent. She would still discuss adult-related issues with her friends and look for solutions on the Internet, until one day I designed a strategy specifically for her and other teens, too. She is now in college, has a good job, knows how to manage her finances: saves, invests, manages expenditures, and has no debt. She also bought her own (brand new) car (Daddy didn't buy it), while accomplishing many other goals. Was it easy—hell no, but definitely worth it big-time.

She Has the Power

She has the power to make whatever she wants out of her life. Life is so precious. Why waste it? I know it sounds like a cliché, but I would tell her constantly, "Be all you can be, Alex. Challenge yourself, get on it; what are you waiting for?"

If she refuses to accept anything but the best, she'll always get the best. She has no idea how much power her mind and body possess; if trained properly, she can take on anything. She should never underestimate the power of her mind.

Come on, get off your rear end and do something with your life! God gave you the tools. Why not use them to their utmost, do not just sit there and exist. To subsist is boring. Go for it! What do you have to lose?

About the Authors

Harris Kern

Harris Kern is one of the world's leading personal mentors (www.disciplinementor.com) and organization performance mentors (www.disciplinetheorganization.com). He is a frequent speaker at business, leadership, and management conferences. His passion is to help people excel in their professional and personal life by developing their self-discipline skills to combat the top issues: severe procrastination, poor time management, ineffective goal management, lack of focus, no sense of urgency, and lack of motivation. He also helps individuals improve their leadership and EQ skills (communication, relationship management, and interpersonal). He pioneered the *Discipline Mentoring Program and Professional/Personal Growth Program (P2GP)*.

Mr. Kern is also the author of over 40 books; some of the titles include:

- *Discipline: Six Steps to Unleashing Your Hidden Potential*
- *Discipline: Training the Mind to Manage Your Life*
- *Discipline: Mentoring Children For Success*
- *Discipline: Take Control of Your Life*

- *Going From Undisciplined to Self-Mastery: Five Simple Steps to Get You There*
- *On Being a Workaholic: Using Balance and Discipline to Live a Better and More Efficient Life.*
- *Live Like You Are Dying: Make Your Life Count Moment By Moment*

Mr. Kern is recognized as the foremost authority on providing practical guidance for solving management issues and challenges. He has devoted over 30 years helping professionals build competitive organizations. His client list reads like a who's who of American and International Business: Standard and Poor's, GE, The Weather Channel, NEWS Corporation, Hong Kong Air Cargo Terminal (HACTL), among dozens of other Fortune 500 and Global 2000 companies.

Mr. Kern is the founder and driving force behind the Enterprise Computing Institute (www.harriskern.com) and the best-selling series of Information Technology (IT) books published by Prentice Hall/Pearson. As founder of the Enterprise Computing Institute, he has brought together the industry's leading minds to publish "how-to" textbooks on the critical issues the IT industry faces.

The series includes titles such as:

- *IT Services*
- *CIO Wisdom, CIO Wisdom II*
- *Managing IT as an Investment, among others.*

Mr. Kern's goal is to arm individuals and organizations with the tools to empower them to become more productive and successful.

Additional Personal Information

Mr. Kern lives every day with a *sense of urgency*! Life is short, and he makes use of every minute, NOT hour or day! Mr. Kern has been productive and successful for over forty years.

He pushes himself extremely hard (by choice):

- Exercises every day of the year

- Traveled to every continent and hundreds of cities all over the world (some several times)
- Established several successful businesses
- Purchased his first home at the age of 19 in the San Francisco Bay area
- Raised a wonderful family
- Trained his mind and body to sleep 4 hours a night
- Financially set at the age of 38
- Dawned the cover of *Hot Rod Magazine* with his muscle car and speed boat at the age of 21 (July 1975 issue)
- Climbed the corporate ladder of a multibillion-dollar company without a formal college education at the age of 31
- Published dozens of books through his own imprint with the largest publishing company in the world

Most people would consider his daily routine crazy and unhealthy; however, Mr. Kern is 62 years old, and he has mastered the ultimate level of discipline since his early twenties. Mr. Kern believes that the body and mind should be pushed to the max every single day. The difference is he has the experience to do so; however, Mr. Kern would never push his clients in this manner unless of course this is their wish.

Mr. Kern's greatest assets are his caring demeanor, incomparable energy, and desire to help people manage their life efficiently. He wants to help as many people as possible fulfill their goals and aspirations.

Acknowledgments

- A special thank you to my business colleague and close friend Leticia Gomez for strategizing with me to develop the premise for this book.
- To my daughter, Alex, for her unconditional love.
- To my wife, Mayra, who I adore and love immensely until the last breath I inhale on this planet.

Ina D'Aleo

Ina D'Aleo is an early childhood special education teacher who has been working in the education field since 2007. She lives in New York City.

Acknowledgements

- I didn't fully acknowledge and understand how difficult it is to be a parent until I became one myself. I love being a mom to you, my dear son Alex. Like all the children of your age you have your weakness for tech gadgets, but it's my hope that one day you will turn your weakness into strength and become what you want to be. My most important goal is to love, support and be there for you. I love being a mom to you. The best feeling is seeing you happy and fulfilled.
- Harris, thank you for fulfilling my vision of making this book possible. Without a doubt, you were the key to making this book what it is due to your unusual level of dedication and hard work. When you work, you work really hard, and you consistently hold yourself to a high standard. You are the one who influenced me with your writing and inspired me to master my life using discipline as a powerful tool. I am so happy that I came across you. Thank you for making such a valuable contribution in my life.

Dr. Joseph Avant

I graduated the University of North Texas (UNT) with a double major in math and history. I then taught high school math for 4 years. Then I decided to return to UNT to pursue the study of philosophy. After 2 years of that, I was accepted into the masters program in humanities at the University of Dallas (UD, not UTD). The concentration of my masters in humanities was politics. I was then accepted into UD's philosophy PhD program. The area of expertise in my PhD is the relation between Classical (Plato & Aristotle) and postmodern (Nietzsche & Heidegger). My dissertation is on Plato's longest dialogue, the Laws. The significance of this for our present purposes is that literally the first great philosophical essay on the problem of technology was written by Heidegger and, as I contend, all of it was foreseen by Plato, particularly in the Laws. More specifically, the entirety of Plato's Laws fundamentally concerns the proper way in which to educate the youth with a vigilant eye toward the detrimental effects of innovation (aka "technology").

Bibliography

Abraham, K. and Studaker-Cordner, M. (2015). *Smart but Helpless Kids: Can Your Child Make It in the Real World?* Retrieved from http://www.empoweringparents.com/teaching-life-skills-kids-teens.php

Buchanan, R.A. (2015). *History of Technology.* Retrieved from http://www.britannica.com/technology/history-of-technology

Davidson, S.N. (2012). *Now You See It: How Technology and Brain Science Will Transform Schools and Business for the 21st Century.* New York: Penguin Books.

Freed, R. (2015). *Wired Child: Debunking Popular Technology Myths.* South Carolina: CreateSpace Independent Publishing Platform.

Gardner, H. and Davis, K. (2013). *The App Generation: How Today's Youth Navigate Identity, Intimacy, and Imagination in a Digital World.* New Haven and London: Yale University Press.

Glassier, W. (2002). *Unhappy Teenagers: A Way for Parents and Teachers to Reach Them.* New York: HarperCollins Publishers.

Kutscher, M.L. and Moran, M. (2009). *Organizing the Disorganized Child: Simple Strategies to Succeed in School.* New York: HarperCollins Publishers.

Lehart, A. (2015). *Teens, Social Media, and Technology Overview.* Retrieved from http://www.pewinternet.org

Lender, W.L. (2014). *A Practical Guide to Parenting in the Digital Age: How to Nurture Safe, Balanced, and Connected Children and Teens.* South Carolina: CreateSpace independent Publishing Platform.

Morrison, G.S. (2011). *Early Childhood Education Today.* Upper Saddle River, New Jersey, Columbus, Ohio: Pearson.

Pan, J. (2012). *Social Media-Connected Teens Seek Time Offline [Study].* Retrieved from http://mashable.com/2012/06/25/social-media-teens/

Prensky, M. (2011). *Digital Natives, Digital Immigrants.* Retrieved from http://www.marcprensky.com/writing/Prensky

Pressman-Donaldson, S., Jackson R., Dr. Pressman, R.M. (2014). *The Learning Habit: A Groundbreaking Approach to Homework and Parenting That Helps Our Children Succeed in School and Life.* New York: Perigee Books.

Steinberg, S. and Riehl, J. (2012). *Technology and Kids: A High-Tech Parenting Guide.* READ.ME.

Steiner-Adair, C. and Barker, T.H. (2014). *The Big Disconnect: Protecting Childhood and Family Relationships in the Digital Age.* New York: Harper Paperbacks.

Summers, P. and DeSollar, A. (2013). *Toddlers on Technology: A Parents' Guide.* Bloominghton, Indiana: AuthorHouse.

Theoharis, M. (2012). *Teen Sexting.* Retrieved from http://www.criminaldefenselawyer.com/crime-penalties/juvenile/sexting.htm

Wallace, K. (2015). *The Real Parenting Lessons of the 'Child Predator Social Experiment'*. Retrieved from http://www.cnn.com/2015/08/20/health/child-predator-video-parenting-lessons/

Zimbardo, P. and Coulombe N.D. (2015). *Man Disconnected: How Technology Has Sabotaged What It Means to Be Male*. Ebury Digital.

CPSIA information can be obtained
at www.ICGtesting.com
Printed in the USA
LVOW04*2256150916

504847LV00008B/46/P